"Today we are receiving a veritable ocean of cos... rarity to find a genuine light language channel w... schema of Pleiadian healing potential. Pavlina's channel provides a written language for her transmissions, and it is clear that her work has a deft and original touch. For her techniques have purity, simplicity, and grace arising from them—by which one can feel the gentle yet penetrative power of this star system's intelligence and teaching. After all, our extraterrestrial galactic companions are all too aware of how complicated and clumsy we humans can be with our own healing. I so look forward to observing the evolving facets of Pavlina's beautiful work."

— **STEWART PEARCE**, master of voice, angelic emissary, and author of
The Alchemy of Voice and *Angels of Atlantis Oracle Cards*

"A heart-centered book filled with Pleiadian messages to awaken humanity from a deep sleep and guide them to cosmic freedom. Pavlina Klemm presents Pleiadian teaching on how chakras receive the frequency of the Divine Source and how we can consciously, through various exercises, activate and sustain this frequency in the body. An introduction to the Cosmic Pharmacy, healing number sequences, and detailed descriptions of how to work with them are a great addition to any healer's toolbox. You must read the book to understand the connection between bees, honey, and the Pleiades. Once it clicks in your mind, your heart will be overfilled with love and sweetness. Pavlina's light messages from the Pleiades encourage us to continue overcoming our current challenges while envisioning the best possible future for humankind. This is the book you will want to keep in your library."

— **EVA MARQUEZ**, healer, teacher, and author of
Activate Your Cosmic DNA and *Pleiadian Code*

"Cosmic consciousness opens your world and your heart. With uplifting, channeled messages and exercises, Pavlina offers you keys for activating healing frequencies in your body, chakras, heart, and energy through affirmations, visualizations, and numerology. Her radiant light, love, and conviction help you sustain your own. Read this book to build hope, embrace the whole of your light field, and expand your consciousness. Read it to receive the gift of healing words from our star teachers."

— **MEG BEELER**, shamanic guide and author of
Weave the Heart of the Universe into Your Life

LIGHT MESSAGES
FROM THE
PLEIADES

A NEW MATRIX OF GALACTIC ORDER

Pavlina Klemm

Translated by
Hilary Snellgrove

FINDHORN PRESS

Findhorn Press
One Park Street
Rochester, Vermont 05767
www.findhornpress.com

Text stock is SFI certified

Findhorn Press is a division of Inner Traditions International

Originally published in German by AMRA Verlag & Records as
Lichtbotschaften von den Plejaden 7: Wissen für die Neue Zeit

Disclaimer
The information in this book is given in good faith and intended for information
only. Neither author nor publisher can be held liable by any person for any loss
or damage whatsoever which may arise from the use of this book or any of the
information therein.

Cataloging-in-Publication data for this title is available from the Library of Congress

ISBN 978-1-64411-825-2 (print)
ISBN 978-1-64411-826-9 (ebook)

Printed and bound in the United States by Lake Book Manufacturing, LLC
The text stock is SFI certified. The Sustainable Forestry Initiative® program
promotes sustainable forest management.

10 9 8 7 6 5 4 3 2 1

Edited by Nicky Leach
Cover and interior illustration by Josephine Wall, www.josephinewall.co.uk
Text design, layout and illustrations by Damian Keenan
This book was typeset in Adobe Garamond Pro, Calluna Sans and with
ITC Century Std used as a display typeface.

To send correspondence to the author of this book, mail a first-class letter to the
author c/o Inner Traditions • Bear & Company, One Park Street, Rochester,
VT 05767, and we will forward the communication, or contact the author directly
at **https://pavlina-klemm.com**

Contents

PART TWO
Messages from the Pleiadians on the Current Situation

Preface

Dear reader of these light-filled messages!

This book was written in a time pertaining to one of the most important human epochs. The Pleiadians have pointed out to us, time and again, that we are approaching a "light-filled revolution," but the expectations and anticipations we had of this time have been far exceeded.

I think very few people imagined that this time would be so turbulent and revolutionary. Who would have expected that cosmic processes would affect us so intensively and that processes involving the human community would happen so quickly?

Inexorably and with seven-mile strides we are approaching the structure of the new life of the human community. Inexorably and with seven-mile strides we are approaching the new cosmic light frequencies that connect us to previously unimaginable possibilities. Inexorably and with seven-mile strides we are approaching the expansion in consciousness of the whole of humanity. Every day, new information comes to us and enters the hearts and systems of we human beings.

Everyone who chose to incarnate at this time on this Earth was in agreement with this great, cosmic, divine plan. Everyone knew beforehand what was going to happen on this planet. Our minds merely caused us to forget this when we incarnated on the Earth.

We are all in the "same boat," and in this incarnation we are now faced with one of the greatest tasks of all our incarnations so far on this planet. It is our task to allow our hearts to shine and to connect the light of our hearts with other human beings' lights and with the lights of other cosmic events. Every radiant, illuminated, and pure heart is incredibly important! Every radiant, illuminated, and pure heart increases the light of the overall development of humanity!

At this time, it is essential to remember how great the light is that we carry within us. It is essential to forgive all those who have harmed us, to ask forgiveness of all those whom we have harmed. And above all—to forgive ourselves. Make peace with other people, souls, and beings and make peace with yourself! Make peace with all that we have done to each other in the most diverse karmic situations and the means by which we have harmed each other.

I have never been more grateful to the Pleiadian beings for accompanying us and passing on information that helps us to survive in these turbulent and revolutionary times. If we accept their help—for which they expect nothing from us in return, nothing at all—then we can live through this time easily and trustingly, with effortless staying power.

I feel their presence, I feel their light and their wisdom. The Pleiadians are part of my family. They have continuous understanding for me, they pass on healing impulses to me and they allow me to see this world as it really is. In their presence, my intuition is always considerably more pronounced, enabling me to take the path that is best for me. My self-love, which enables me to see the world without judgment and without feelings of resentment, is always considerably more pronounced in their presence.

I know that I chose this incarnation myself. I know that this incarnation, precisely at this time, offers healing and detachment from the last karmic causation I have accumulated here on Earth. We have all been given this opportunity. We have been given the opportunity to discard everything we no longer want to carry around with us. Many of us, including me, have chosen to take this precious opportunity.

Everything is becoming more subtle. Subtlety is increasing every day. The cosmic frequencies coming to the Earth are vibrating ever higher and faster. Everything is proceeding in a natural, cosmic process. And we human beings are going through this process.

Our systems are purifying themselves of thousands of years of imprisonment in a matrix that did not have our well-being in mind.

This we may now discard—and this book helps us to understand. It helps us to understand the overall situation we were in and it helps us to completely heal our whole system.

And once again, we have tremendous help: this book is charged with the new frequencies of the positive future—every single word!

The positive frequencies that accompany this book are not yet to be found on our planet. They enable us to heal our systems more easily and more quickly with no burdening, negative accompanying frequencies, and they also enable us to let go of the reality of the past if we allow for this possibility. You will feel the lightness of these frequencies.

The words of the individual exercises in this book carry the positive light information of the future of humanity, enabling our human system to regenerate more strongly—so that the system can finally recover from the strains of the manipulated past.

The Pleiadian beings have received permission from the cosmic Council of Light and from divine intelligence to work with us energetically and to support us. The manipulation of humanity by the dark beings and forces was too strong for us to be able to help ourselves in every situation on this planet.

For this I am grateful to the Pleiadian beings. I bless their presence and their existence. I bless the presence and existence of all of you!

I wish you much joy, new insights, and further healing impulses for your soul, for your mind, and for your body. My wish for you is that, through your personal healing, the systems of your families will also heal; and that your relationships and opinions about people who play the role of your adversary in this incarnation heal, or otherwise reflect or mirror to you qualities that you have not yet been able to discard.

"Step by step," as the Pleiadians like to say, we are moving toward a positive future. Everyone for themselves and everyone as part of the human community.

Let us kindle the light in our hearts and together illuminate our human reality.

Our hearts connect us. Our hearts heal us.

With love and gratitude!
Your Pavlina

Greetings from the Pleiadian Civilization

Dear messengers of light! We are delighted to be able to enter your time frame and share more information with you. Only a tiny fraction of your Earthly time has passed since our last encounter. For us, these encounters with you are truly heart-warming every time, and we enter your reality with great gratitude. We fill your hearts with our joy and happiness. We are glad that our communication is yielding enormous, positive results!

Huge morphogenetic fields have formed around every single reader. Huge morphogenetic fields have formed between you and all other fields of consciousness. A great light has unfolded between you and the advocates of cosmic light information, impulses, frequencies, and energies—huge fields that connect us.

Your heart and consciousness power have created portals of light between planet Earth and our Pleiadian stars. Expansive fields were formed between the Earth and the other stars and planets from which you originated. You have amplified the light of your heart, the light of your body and your aura many times over.

Thanks to your consciousness work, your cells have begun to connect to the consciousness of the divine Central Sun, to the consciousness of the infinite divine power, to love, energy, beauty, and diversity.

Your spiritual knowledge has increased considerably and your knowledge is now connecting with the knowledge of other human individuals who have found a home here on this planet for their incarnation. Through this, you support each other and your light vibration increases.

The overall light on your planet is increasing. It literally intensifies day by day. Every day, you move closer and closer to the Golden Age.

The Golden Age for the human community.

The Golden Age for the kingdoms of nature.

The Golden Age for planet Earth.

The Golden Age for other inhabited planets and their civilizations that exist in the same time and space of your shared galaxy.

Events on planet Earth gathered speed significantly at the beginning of the year 2020. Everything is being illuminated, the darkness is diminishing and the dark forces know full well that their time on this beautiful planet is coming to an end. They know full well that the inflowing golden frequencies do not align with their mental and existential reality and their matrix.

The great worldwide movement initiated by the dark powers and beings literally froze the entire human population.

And they are still trying to spread their plans and their nets into every corner of this planet and into every thought and emotion of individual human beings.

Time and again in previous books, we told you that a time will come when the mass media will also reveal its entirely negative power. We advised you to be careful, to form your own opinions, and to listen to your intuition.

Many of you have followed this advice and have not let yourselves be thrown off balance. However, many human beings have lost their positive view of the future and have lost their way.

With this book, we would like to help you to fine-tune your own opinion and to feel your intuition more clearly. For this, we would like to offer you energy exercises to help you purify yourself from this difficult reality and from humanity's dark past, exercises to help you to heal the energy systems of your chakras.

Your chakras are direct gateways to the Divine Source and all its information and frequencies. Your chakras connect you to the light and love of the cosmos.

We will move forward with you step by step. We will accompany you and help you to understand your reality. Being near you gives us great joy. We are very often close to you and observing what is happening.

That gives us great pleasure.

Even though tremendous processes are taking place behind the scenes of the events of worldwide evolution, which will lead to the overall liberation of humanity from enslavement by the dark forces, we are not yet allowed by divine intelligence and by the Highest Cosmic Council to appear completely physically in your human reality and temporal presence.

The required consciousness development of human beings must reach at least 30 to 40 percent of the population in order for humanity to truly be able to grasp and comprehend the overall situation as it is right now—the overall situation with all its impacts and causes. Once consciousness development has reached at least 30 percent of the population, this consciousness will be transmitted further, through the morphogenetic fields created with the help of pure human hearts.

The number of people whose hearts are now shining brightly, the number of people needed for the successful ascent into the Golden Age was reached at the end of 2018 and the beginning of 2019. A magnificent development...

The important thing now is how many human beings are still going to awaken from their long sleep and connect consciously to the morphogenetic fields of humanity that are helping to liberate people on all levels of their being.

The process that started at the beginning of 2020 brings with it very significant changes that will create a positive future. Even if this time is difficult, chaotic, and turbulent, thanks to this phase humanity will experience an increase in its spiritual consciousness.

And opportunities will open up for humanity that individuals would never have dared to imagine in their wildest dreams—opportunities that will help humanity to live in happiness and harmony.

This time brings about the fall of all those structures that no longer serve humanity. This time brings about the final departure of those beings who harm humanity. This time brings about the awakening of humanity out of its sleep and rigidity.

A time such as this in which you now find yourselves has never before been experienced by humankind.

Humankind has never known a comparable situation. There will be a universal awakening and a universal purification of every negative structure in the whole community and in each individual. Every human being will feel what their task is at this time. Every human being will receive impulses from divine intelligence, enabling them to recognize what does not belong to their true reality.

We ask you all for greater endurance and for your understanding of your situation. We ask you to give up everything negative that does not belong to you. Your perseverance will be rewarded with the freedom that will follow, and with the matrix of your system fitting into the system of this galaxy.

Every one of you planned your incarnation here on this planet and every one of you was in agreement with the precise plan and with the precise course of your incarnation before your arrival on Earth. Perhaps you can recall this in moments when you feel that the strength and the motivation to continue on your path seem to be deserting you.

Every one of you has had conversations with your light companions and with your non-incarnated family members in the heaven of human beings. Every one of you has had conversations with the cosmic Council of Light and every one of you has chosen to process your burdensome issues, has chosen to help other people or beings... has chosen to find freedom in your heart—each according to their development and their possibilities.

Even if not every human mind remembers their heavenly plan, a great common intention connects every human being on this planet. And that is to remember their own divine essence, the divine essence of their own soul, the liberation of their own person, and the liberation of the human community.

Every one, truly every single one of you is part of this plan. Each and every one who has come to this planet—in this time and in this space.

Be certain that every single one of you already knew before coming to this planet that the liberation of humanity would succeed. Every single one of you knew what the earthly path to liberation would be like.

The current situation is one of the last attempts by the dark forces to drive humanity back into the clutches of dark reality. You were, however, informed also about this situation in the heavenly dimension.

Every one of you who chose this present incarnation acted very courageously. And every one of you has had heightened frequencies of cosmic freedom introduced into your system from the light world, which will help you to free yourselves from the clutches of the dark forces. It is enough to remember this fact—and you are already connected to the frequencies of cosmic freedom!

Become aware of your power and become aware of this gift that was given to you on your arrival on the Earth—that was given to all of you.

Cosmic freedom! That is the cosmic key for the final, concluding phase of the evolution of the human being!

Become aware, every single one of you, that the frequency of cosmic freedom is available to you at all times. You only need to anchor this frequency in your heart to be able to go through this incarnation more easily, with an overall view and with peaceful but at the same time clear deliberation!

Remember this truth: every one of you had the opportunity before this incarnation on the Earth to ask for an increased number of light beings to accompany and protect them during this incarnation. If you have forgotten this fact, summon as many light beings as you need, right now! Call on the angels of peace! They bring peace to your heart and to your life. They bring peace to the hearts and lives of your loved ones when they remember that they are accompanied by angels of peace in this planetary incarnation!

We look forward to accompanying you further along the path. We look forward to being close to you. We look forward to more human beings remembering their essence through these words and thereby raising their consciousness. Remember, their awareness contributes to the percentage increase in the number of people necessary for the overall liberation of the human community.

We look forward to working with you and to the feeling that arises when we connect with each other and when we meet on the level of the purest human divine essence!

We look forward to more adventures with you!

We look forward to your wonderful future!

Your Pleiadian Community

PART ONE

Messages and Exercises
for the New Era

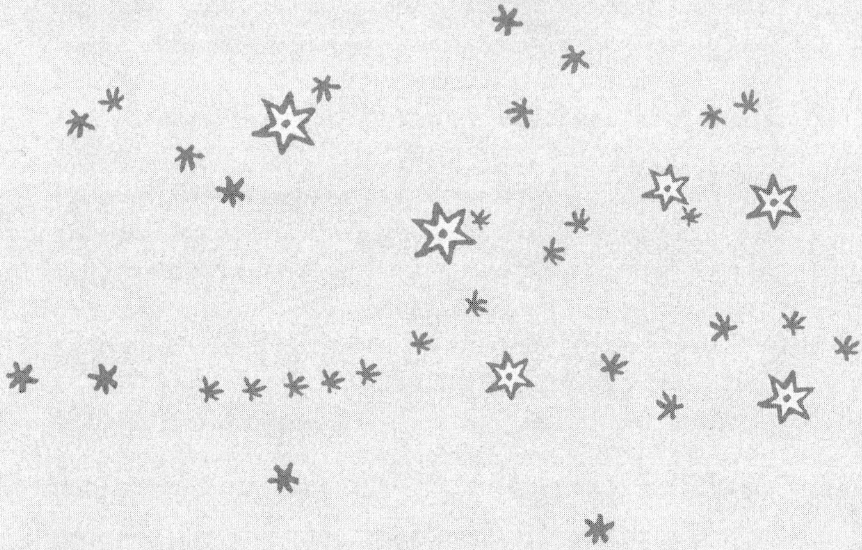

1

The Power of the
Human Heart

We had no idea that the power of each single human being's heart would be so great. We had no idea that human beings were capable of kindling such great light within themselves, able to shine through every reality of the human being.

We knew that human beings were immensely radiant and energetically powerful, but we had no idea that after the expansion of the individual's consciousness, their personal light would shine so magically and so powerfully!

We have heard of the radiant human heart many times in conversations with members of the Cosmic Council. We have been lovingly told many times that a human heart that radiates has such power that it can connect dimensions, spaces, and times with other human beings who radiate the same frequency. The power and light of the human heart is spoken of in the Cosmic Council and among other extraterrestrial civilizations as a phenomenon that every one of us wishes to observe and feel. This is another reason why so many souls incarnate into human bodies. The human heart is a phenomenon and it is almost unbelievable what human love can do to the human heart, how far and how powerfully this light expands when the human being is in love, how beautifully the heart and the whole being of this person shine!

During this time there is an increased light vibration of the heart organ and its cell quality is augmented. The cells in the heart are the first in the human body to connect, at least partially, to the divine intelligence and to the divine light with all its information. The cells in the heart are pioneers and a model for the other cells of the human body.

The cells in the heart that have already completely and fully connected to the divine light and its information have become independent universes within the human heart. Every single cell in the human heart that is connected to the divine light carries the intelligence of the Divine Source within itself!

In this way, the human heart is connected to the Divine Source and to its information, light, and energy; and love flows to it continuously!

Every illuminated cell of the human heart carries divine consciousness. In every cell there is information about our origin and our entire existence. Each cell in the heart is a single, independent world and yet the worlds of the illuminated cells are interconnected.

Every photon—light particle—of the divine light carries within itself all the information concerning all the events and origins of this infinite universe. Every photon originated in the Divine Source and is forever connected to the Divine Source through its intelligence and light. Your illuminated heart cells can receive and decipher the information of the Divine Source!

The human heart, as a divine organ, is able to communicate continuously with the Divine Source. Each illuminated cell expands its consciousness, causing the light of the heart organ to intensify more and more. Each human heart has its own consciousness and contains its own information, and the consciousness of the Divine Source connects it with the information in the divine frequencies.

Almost every human individual speaks to their heart as one whole organ. But you could, if you wanted to, also talk to every single cell, because every single cell has its own consciousness and intelligence.

The cells of your heart are connected to the vast, energetic morphogenetic fields of your human hearts. There are countless morphogenetic fields of human hearts. The respective light frequency of the heart decides to which energetic morphogenetic field the individual connects. And every human being has the possibility to connect with every field.

24

The extent to which they positively change their existence and their thinking is at the sole discretion of the individual. The purest morphogenetic fields of human hearts are connected to the purest essence of the Divine Source.

Human individuals with radiant and illuminated hearts and pure thoughts vibrate at a very high frequency of light and connect to the purest energetic morphogenetic fields of humanity. The illuminated cells, which are connected with the purest Divine Source, pass on their consciousness, light, and information to other cells in the human body. A chain reaction then occurs within the cells.

However, not all cells of the individual parts or organs of the body are currently able to raise their frequency and expand their consciousness. Individual parts or organs of the body have their own consciousness and have had individual experiences from past times or incarnations. Therefore, individual organs are connected to the different cosmic morphogenetic fields of those specific organs and to the fields of experience of the respective human individual.

Each organ in the human body vibrates at a different color frequency. Each organ is also connected to the cosmic tone, which provides vital energy to the organs. Therefore, we would like to give you information here that will help your individual organs to raise their frequency and find healing, so that the consciousness, the intelligence, and the light of the heart cells are also transferred to them.

If the organs carry burdensome emotions and thoughts, it is not possible for them to absorb the consciousness, intelligence, and light of the heart cells. If a human being carries burdensome emotions and thoughts, their body is not able to initiate the process of the light body—so then this is not activated. The light chakras located above the head of the human being do receive that person's primal information and the primal frequencies of the Divine Source, but their body is not yet able to receive the purest divine energy.

In the earlier books, we went through the process with you, step by step, and together we purified your heart and negative aspects. We will continue to work with you to enable human material substance to experience its full connection to the Divine Source. We will continue to move forward with you so that your material substance can heal completely and connect through its cellular light with the purest fields of the divine world.

Peace with you, peace with us!

2

Introduction to the World of the
Chakras and Their Consciousness

The power of your heart is enormous. The power of your heart heals and harmonizes all the spaces and times of your reality. And it is precisely this power of the heart that will also help you in the further steps of your spiritual healing.

The power and love of the heart, coming from the Divine Source, is an engine. It gives you life energy and a connection to yourself, a connection with your body, your mind, and your soul. In this book, you will often use the power and love of your heart to heal other areas of yourself.

In the last book, we described the chakras and their function for the first time. We shared brief information with you to help you to reprogram issues and problems that are locked in your chakras. In the following chapters we will give you specific exercises to enable your chakras to work well.

After purifying and reprogramming your chakras to positivity, you free your soul and mind. Your organs connect to those cosmic morphogenetic fields that are responsible for the individual organs. Your organs will be able to communicate with cosmic intelligence. Life energy will flow to your organs continuously via the morphogenetic fields.

Human beings who incarnate on this planet called Earth bring with them their complete connection to the systems of the surrounding planets and to the systems of this galaxy. When they incarnate, they are additionally connected to the systems of planet Earth.

Burdens that human beings have accumulated over the period of their incarnations on Earth upset their matrix order, and the energetic system of the human being begins to collapse. This is because they have brought with them burdens from past incarnations. Entire information systems were transferred to human beings via morphogenetic fields. One could say that they constantly move with a human being from incarnation to incarnation until that human being either notices them or falls ill and starts doing something about this negative information. As long as they go unnoticed by the human being, they stay close or inhabit certain dimensions, times and spaces of that human being's reality.

Negative burdens—which we have informed you about again and again—can cause great damage in the life of each individual human being and likewise in the overall existence of the human community, as all human beings are interconnected. But fortunately, human beings also carry all the positive information gathered from incarnation to incarnation, which makes it easier for them to free themselves from negative burdens. The present time is important for the process of energetic restoration, enabling this to reflect positively in the physical events happening around the human being.

In earlier times, no one noticed the negative information in their system and they simply accepted their fate, which often did not look particularly rosy. But now, in this time, many of the inhabitants of this planet are waking up and realizing that an energetic restoration of their own existence and the existence of humanity is unavoidable. And every human being who takes steps to heal their own reality is also contributing to the healing of the reality of humankind.

Do you understand? When an individual human being connects with the fields of consciousness of their own immaculate existence, the systems of other human beings begin to heal. In this way, you heal each other. In this way, humanity will gradually be able to return to its essence and to its perfect order.

Our connection to the surrounding planets and their systems in terms of frequency and light is immeasurably important. Such a connection is essential for the overall system and the overall formation of a human being. When human beings learn to absorb the energy coming from the cosmos, it gives them energetic power. The importance of the light and the frequencies of the planets that give energetic power to the human body should never be forgotten. Good reception of cosmic life energy is essential for the optimal functioning of the chakras.

Well-functioning chakras help you in your consciousness development. Information from the divine intelligence can then flow specifically to you and your chakras can decipher it more easily. Your chakras are like deciphering, light-filled "organs" for information from divine intelligence.

Until now, the chakras of the human body have been more or less clogged and polluted with the problems and issues of earthly incarnations. If they function well, this accelerates your personal spiritual development of consciousness, because the light information coming to the chakras can immediately communicate with the soul, mind, and body of the human being.

The original function of the chakras—that is, to receive light information—will again become possible.

As your chakras turn, the light in them forms spirals. Every rotation of your chakras connects you helically with other worlds and universes pertaining to your existence as well as with the entire existence of infinity. Each chakra is a gateway to other worlds of your existence that you may have known nothing about. Each chakra is a gateway that opens when the blockages of old, faulty programs have been released. But chakras are also gateways to the worlds of your unprocessed issues or emotions and other energy fields that connect you to these negativities.

In a blocked chakra, however, energy does not rotate in a spiral. In most cases, the energy is then almost static, immobile. This immobility prevents you from connecting and moving with the infinitude of the infinite happening of universal existence. But, if they are functioning well, your chakras are light portals through which you can travel virtually to other worlds and other realities. To do this, it is enough to connect with the individual chakra— the portal.

Each chakra enables you to enter worlds of different dimensions. You can virtually travel through them into the past and into the future. You can do this with their help, but you can also use the power of the moment and connect with your presence.

The portals of your chakras connect you to your soul, your mind, your body, and to the wider happenings of your subtle and physical world. As you connect through your chakras, you enter realities that are there for your healing that you would never have dared to dream of. It is enough to enter the space of the individual chakra.

As you may know, each chakra has its own characteristic color and vibration. If the circumstances are positive, the worlds in your chakras have exactly this characteristic color and vibration. Under negative circumstances, when issues have remained unprocessed, they are stored in the memory of those chakras that correspond to them in color and vibration. This happens with unprocessed issues from your past incarnations just as it happens with unprocessed issues from the past of this incarnation. They are stored in the memory of particular chakras. And it is not only the vibration of your unprocessed emotions and thoughts that is then stored in these chakras, it is also the unprocessed issues of other people with whom you have had something to do in the course of your life.

If you learn to move between the gateways of your chakras and to perceive information of whatever kind, you will find that the worlds contained within them connect with the worlds of other people or beings and that these again connect with the worlds of even more people and beings who bear similar issues. As you move into the worlds of your illuminated and healed chakras, you connect with the most beautiful spaces of light and kingdoms of nature, in wonderful colors, forms, and light frequencies that are populated by light beings. And these beings connect you with further wonderful light beings and light worlds.

The world of your chakras connects you to your inner world and to your inner life, which is equally connected to the surrounding light world and to the surrounding physical life. You literally carry within you the connection to your own universe, which connects you to the universe of the Divine Source.

The world of your illuminated chakras connects you with your illuminated future here on Earth and with the future of your existence in the heaven of human beings or your personal light-filled home. You could say that by working on your chakras you create favorable conditions for your stay in your light home after you leave your physical sheath. You create worlds of light for yourselves, which will be shown to you instantly by the beings of light after you leave this planet—worlds in which your rest in the heavenly dimensions will be peaceful.

All the energy work you do is encoded in your system, every positive thought and emotion. Everything positive helps you to heal your future here on Earth and the future in your light world.

Your energy work helps you to finally lighten the heavy backpack of your destiny that you have carried from incarnation to incarnation. It helps to make your present and subsequent incarnations more enlightened, joyful, and happy.

Peace with you, peace with us!

3

Orella and Her Message, "The Truth Will Prevail"

That chakras are gateways into inner worlds and into the spaces of one's own knowing was already spoken of in your ancient myths. But that each and every one of you is a key to the ancient knowledge that humanity longs for was forgotten. Each one of you holds the key to your knowledge, to the knowledge of the Divine Source, and to knowledge in its entirety. Each one of you is therefore a key to the transition into the positive future of the human community.

At this time, you are all becoming conscious again of that precious key that opens the door to the positive future on this planet.

Every human being who has found at least some part of the truth of the divine intelligence and some part of the truth about the history and the true knowledge of the human community has initiated their personal timeline, which was developed for the human community by divine intelligence.

The timeline created by the dark forces, meant to lead the human community to destruction, no longer exists. Around Easter of the year 2020, it was transformed.

Divine intelligence has created a new timeline that allows humanity to grow and develop in a way that serves humanity. This timeline is still very chaotic at the moment, because the old non-functioning systems created by the dark forces must first be overthrown in order for stable systems to be created again. But this new timeline not only brings humanity great positive changes, it also brings back the lost knowledge that forms the basis for the human community to develop successfully and in the right direction.

Many people and beings are searching for the ancient knowledge of Lemuria and Atlantis. They are looking for knowledge from those times when human beings mastered telepathy and teleportation and could mentally move objects.

Many people have forgotten that this knowledge is hidden in their energy body, in their systems and chakras, and that each one of them has access to it. It has been stored in various "dimension strands" that human beings can call up at any time. But in order for you to become your own key to your own knowledge and to the knowledge of the human collective as well as to the knowledge of divine intelligence, it is necessary for you to purify your chakras on the energy level. And your heart!

When you remember, at least in part, your own divine essence, that divine essence that each of you carries within you, it brings back the memory of your own divine truth and your own intuition.

Manipulation has increased so much lately that it is necessary for you to purify your chakras. It is only when your intuition connects you to divine truth that manipulation can no longer find a way into your system. In divine truth, manipulation and destructive thoughts do not exist.

The truth that is increasingly coming to the surface at the moment is strengthening the energetic connection with the positive timeline of humanity more and more.

Each one of you carries it within you, the truth, the divine truth, and the intuition.

It is enough to remember who you are.

It is enough to remember why you are here.

It is enough to remember why you came to this planet.

Truth accompanies you throughout your life on Earth and enables you, in the situations you meet in life, to act in the way in which it is important for you to act at that moment. The truth that every human being carries in their system is a rather extraordinary element of the human composition. If it connects with the truth of divine intelligence, it connects you with every event of this infinite universe.

Manipulation has a dark energy. In contrast to the divine truth that each of you carries within you, it vibrates at a very low frequency. Truth, the divine truth and justice have extremely high-frequency light units that turn the key to humanity's positive future.

The truth, which is coming to the surface step by step, will soon spread its light over the whole surface of this beautiful planet. The light of truth kindles the flame of a vast, powerful light in the human heart, which is the first and most important access to the gates of the cosmic world. And at the same time it is a doorway to the collective consciousness of humanity.

The chain reaction that is just about to start will connect individual human beings who have the flame of truth in their hearts, so that a huge energy field is formed that connects with the truth of divine intelligence.

Everyone carries the knowledge and the truth within them, in their system, in their energy body, in their human body. All you need to do is unlock your knowledge!

You have waited so long for this knowledge and have prepared yourselves to connect with the information of your own knowledge and the knowledge of humanity. Through the power of your purified heart and chakras you are now connecting to the morphogenetic fields of your own knowledge, the knowledge of humanity, and the knowledge of divine intelligence. *You yourselves are your key and thus the doorway to all realms of knowledge.*

The matrix of the third level of consciousness will soon depart from the human community. The matrix of limited possibilities for the human soul, mind, and body is leaving planet Earth and its citizens. Easter 2020 was an extremely important milestone in this development.

The third level of consciousness still exists on this planet, but the fifth level of consciousness has already been developed by human beings. The third level will be transformed into light after a certain time. The breakaway from dark manipulation and lies will soon be realized. It depends on how quickly humanity remembers.

Every one of you who has chosen to bring your light and love to this planet is indispensable. Every one of you helps the overall development of humanity.

We thank you now for the work you will be doing in the future for your spiritual development and for your personal remembering, which will also be of benefit to those close to you.

We thank you very much for your decision.

We thank you for feeling addressed on the energy level by this book and for consequently entering into an energetic connection and dialogue with us.

Every one of you who connects to us energetically automatically increases and strengthens their connection to the cosmic world and to the Pleiadian energy.

Above all, however, they increase their love, the most healing and powerful greatness that there is.

We thank you for your help!
Yours, Orella

4

The Chakras, Their Worlds, and Exercises for Their Healing

Let us now move on to the specific healing of your chakras, those energetic organs that enable the passage of information from the subtle to the physical body of the human being. Please be conscious of the fact that the chakras are the basis for healing all the systems of your body, spirit, and soul. They are the basis for the healing of human beings on all levels of their being and all levels of their life.

As life goes on, the chakras absorb destructive energetic information, which always weakens the functioning of the corresponding material organs. Some accumulated problems tend to take root in several chakras at once. Then, emotions and thoughts within the system often flow into each other. It therefore makes sense to always purify all the chakras at the same time and not only focus on the one chakra that you know is restricted in its functioning.

The one exception is energetic implants. They are not included in the healing of your overall system with the help of purified chakras.

They were handed over to human beings by the dark forces. If you look at this problem a little more closely, the energetic implants could not have been transferred to human beings in the first place had their chakras been illuminated. The dark beings used an energetic "loophole" to transfer these implants through which they then penetrated the human system. This loophole made the aura a little more permeable at this point, so that the dark beings could access the system. (A suitable affirmation for the removal of energetic implants can be found in the Bonus Affirmations at the end of this book, see page 186).

We will accompany you on the energy level when you work with your chakras. We will provide you with meditative exercises. *Every word of these exercises will be energetically positively charged and attuned to your vibration. Your intention is essential for your healing.*

You can do the exercises individually or all at once, depending on your intuition. This energetic work is deeply purifying and can therefore be very powerful. This means that you should definitely give yourself time to rest afterwards.

Before each meditative exercise, please write the number sequence **3717** on a piece of paper and keep it close by. You can also transmit it to water: place a glass of water on this row of numbers and let it work for at least three minutes.

Or you can visualize it or say it out loud. This sequence of numbers connects you with our Pleiadian healing energy, with our love and our frequency. In addition, it protects you from unwanted foreign energies when processing certain issues, and it supports you energetically in your healing process. It also connects you to the frequency of trust. Trust is incredibly important at this time.

You can also light a candle so that you are clearly visible to the beings of light.

Activation of the Healing Frequencies in the Chakras of Your Palms

Before each exercise, activate the chakras in your palms to support the healing of your main chakras.

Then place your activated hands on your main chakras. To activate them, rub your palms together until they become warm.

Then turn your palms upwards. Connect with all the light beings who can help you with this activation. Connect with us if you like.

And then speak the following words . . .

"I ask for activation of the cosmic healing frequencies in the chakras of my palms. My intention is pure and clear.

The activation is taking place now and in this space. Time and space are one.

3717.3717.3717.

Thank you, thank you, thank you."

If you wish to, let the light beings and us work for at least three minutes.

Your palms are now activated.

If you now move on to a particular chakra, have a pen and paper ready each time before doing the exercise so that you can record what you feel, perceive or see as you work with the chakra. If you do not receive any conscious information during the exercise, it does not matter. Your mind and soul take in the information that the consciousness of your chakras transmits to you during the exercise, and they will deliver it to you at the right time. Remain in a state of trust.

Before and especially after working with your chakras, it is important to drink a lot of water. Your system will release toxins that are related to the specific issues in your body. Water will help your cells to get rid of accumulated toxins and they can regenerate. Whenever you do energy work, drinking water is especially important.

And now you can begin to purify the chakra of your choice . . .

The Light Chakras under Your Feet

The light chakras under your feet connect you with the wisdom and light of the earth-soul Gaia. They connect you to the knowledge that humanity has encoded into the Earth. At the same time, you are connected through them with the meridians of the Earth sphere and with the crystal networks that connect planet Earth with the crystal networks of this galaxy.

The light chakras connect you with the light beings that are inside the Earth. These also include beings responsible for the crystal realms in the Earth, beings responsible for the subterranean realms of gold and minerals, and countless other beings responsible for all the realms and worlds in the Earth's interior. There are also angels and beings of light in underground cities and a large number of them are responsible for the earth-soul Gaia.

Knowledge and the access to information stored in the Earth has been opening up to the human community since 2021. The information and knowledge for the New Era, which originates from Lemuria and Atlantis, will be made available to humanity by the light beings who guard this knowledge in the light-filled interior of the Earth. It is important for the overall development of humanity that this knowledge is not misused. Communication between Gaia and human beings will constantly increase. Humanity's remembrance of its natural being and essence will enable access to ancient information.

Human beings will increasingly remember their spiritual, light-filled connection with the earth-soul Gaia, which arose at the moment of their incarnation on Earth. Every human being was connected to love, light, and to all information and frequencies when they arrived on this planet. When human beings remember this, their hearts will radiate, creating a heart connection between the human being and the consciousness of Gaia. The light chakras under your feet will shine brightly and absorb her wisdom, her consciousness, and her love.

The purer your heart, the greater the luminous intensity of the light chakras under your feet and the easier the access to information from Gaia. Your pure heart increases the light and energy in all your chakras. Spending time in nature is vital for the good functioning of these chakras.

Exercise for the Light Chakras under Your Feet

Visualize or speak the number sequence **3717** *three times.*

Imagine you are in a place in nature that is completely untouched by humankind. In this place, nature is still pure and untouched.

Breathe deeply in this place and choose to heal the seven light-filled chakras under your feet.

Concentrate on the light, golden-copper-colored chakras under your feet. Observe how these chakras expand luminously. Their light connects you to energy pathways—subtle meridians that enliven your energetic and physical body.

You feel golden lines flowing through your body. Their light connects you with the light beings in the interior of this planet. The light of your chakras also connects you with the morphogenetic fields of the knowledge of humanity, which was deposited by the ancestors of humankind in the subterranean realms long ago.

And now the knowledge of humanity is ascending through your light chakras to your mind. Your mind takes in this knowledge and passes it on to you at the right time.

Unite with the light, the love, and the wisdom of the earth-soul Gaia. Her knowledge also rises through your light chakras to your mind.

Thank Gaia for her existence. Bless her.

And now breathe deeply once again.

Unite with the consciousness of your light chakras.

Observe what kind of world and what kind of light beings are present in the world of your chakras.

Now ask the consciousness of your light chakras . . .

"Do you have a message for me?

What can I do for my consciousness development?

What can I do to connect to the light world and to the positive frequencies within the Earth?

I receive all information with gratitude.

Thank you, thank you, thank you."

Now illuminate the chakras under your feet with golden-copper-colored light to support them energetically. Imagine that there are beautiful, translucent crystals in these seven chakras.
Send out the love of your heart to them.
Bless them and bless yourself on all levels of your being.
Take your time. If you have received information, write it down.

The Root Chakra

The root chakra connects you with the Earth, especially with her surface and with all the kingdoms of nature. It connects you with the elements of the Earth. It connects you with the land as well as with the water surfaces of the Earth. Through this chakra you are connected to the physical interior of the Earth—in contrast to the light chakras under your feet, which connect you to the subtle worlds of the Earth's interior.

The frequency of the Earth is increasing continuously.

This releases and reveals blockages encoded in the root chakra of human beings. Issues come to light that block human beings in their natural healing process and in their trust in the natural, worthy course of their incarnation here on Earth. They are being highlighted more than ever before, because human beings now have the opportunity to regard this as a call and to take a closer look at them. At the root of the issues highlighted is the fear for one's own existence. This was artificially introduced into human beings and, through the increased frequency of the Earth, can now be processed and transformed very quickly in the light and the energy of the Earth.

Fear of the future is encoded in the root chakra. Repetitive patterns of fear of the future constrict this chakra and human beings literally have the "ground pulled out from under their feet." They lose contact with Mother Earth and also lose contact with their life force, which is transmitted to them by Mother Earth. Furthermore, uncertainty as to what earthly life will bring, and low confidence in the future, connect human beings to low vibrational frequencies that have settled on the surface of the Earth. The root chakra transmits these low vibrational frequencies through the spinal cord into the whole system of the human being. If you lack confidence, it is best to use the number sequence **3 7 1 7**.

This helps you to gain strength and the certainty that the passage of your incarnation here on Earth will always be positive. It brings back your confidence—confidence in yourself and in your actions here on Earth.

The root chakra of many people living in big cities is greatly stressed because negative energies accumulated on the surface of the ground and a frequency of fear are held there. This chakra is usually also stressed in people who live in energetically burdened houses, built, for example, on former cemeteries, execution sites or places of ritual. If, in addition, there are human souls in such places who have not yet gone into the light, the overall system of the person concerned will be burdened yet again.

The number sequence **1 3 1** helps with the energetic purification of the root chakra. This connects you with the purity, energy, and healing power of all the water surfaces of this planet, and also with all the light beings of nature and the dolphins, who bring to human beings healing, lightness, and a connection to the Divine Source and its abundance.

Exercise for the Root Chakra

Visualize or speak the number sequence **3 7 1 7** *three times.*
Activate the healing frequencies in your palms.
Then place your hands on your root chakra. Breathe deeply and concentrate on your root chakra.
Through your power of thought, illuminate it with a red light. This color connects you with the power and the energy of the Earth. Call the light-filled nature beings, who connect you with the natural kingdom and its healing power, to you.

Call the dolphins, who help you to illuminate your chakra with the power and purity of the oceans and with the element of water, to you.

131.131.131.

Unite with the Earth through the power of your heart and ask the soul of the Earth, Gaia, to purify your root chakra with the power of her heart. The healing energies of all the light-filled nature beings will come together in your root chakra and purify it.

And then speak the following words . . .

"Now and in this space, I separate myself through the power of my intention from all the burdens, negative emotions and thoughts that have closed my chakra.

Now and in this space, I separate myself from all the frequencies of fear that have been artificially transmitted to me.

Now and in this space, I separate myself from all burdens, from all negative emotions and thoughts, in all times, and in all spaces of my entire existence."

Breathe deeply and let go of all negativity. Concentrate again on your root chakra and unite with its consciousness. Observe what is happening in the world of this chakra and which light beings are present within it.

Now ask the consciousness of your root chakra . . .

"Do you have a message for me?

What can I do for your healing?

What can I do for my consciousness development? I receive all information with gratitude. Thank you, thank you, thank you."

Illuminate this chakra once again with clear red light and imagine that there is a beautiful, translucent red crystal within.

Send out the love of your heart to it.

Bless it and bless yourself on all levels of your being.

Take your time. Write down any information received.

The Sacral Chakra

All women on Earth are connected with each other via the sacral chakra, just as they are connected via their common morphogenetic fields. All men on this planet are connected through this chakra and the common fields of men. Likewise, all children up to the age of about twelve or thirteen are connected via the sacral chakra and the children's corresponding fields. Until this age, children are also still energetically connected to their mother. After that, their paths begin to separate and the children attach themselves to the morphogenetic field of either the Earth's women or men.

In the sacral chakra, all the injuries that human beings have experienced through manipulation, sexual violence and abuse here on Earth are encoded. Unprocessed emotions to do with parents and other immediate family members (sisters and brothers) are also stored in this chakra.

By purifying the sacral chakra, every human being can connect to the cosmic field of the natural feminine or masculine power. It provides human beings with an excellent connection to their ancestors in the heaven of human beings and it can also be used to travel easily to ancestral lineages and the experiences of the ancestors here on Earth.

The act of sexual union between man and woman brings about a perfect union of souls. The soul of the man and that of the woman unite full of light into a whole, and the male and female natural cosmic force absorbs a great deal of light energy at this moment. The majestic masculine and magical feminine cosmic powers become manifest in the full union of the souls of man and woman. In the moment of unity, the partners are then in contact with the light of the Divine Source and receive a vast amount of vital life energy. In the purest sexual connection, all chakras light up. The light is transmitted through the spinal cord and radiates through all the systems of both partners.

Unfortunately, the institution of the Church has spoiled this for human beings, making them believe natural sexual power to be something shameful and indecent. In this way, the dark power of the Church has cut the human community off from the life energy and vitality that partners experience in their loving union. As a result, sexuality has often been reduced to a brief experience of satisfaction, and that too filled with the fear of doing something forbidden or unacceptable.

But the human being's spiritual development at the present time is extraordinary, and the perfect union of souls will certainly soon bear within an incredible, light-filled and physical power once again. The energy that arises during the sexual act is stored in the sexual chakra as well as in the root chakra and spreads into all the systems of both partners at the climax of the act.

By the way, the light-filled, subtle development of the human body will lead to the emergence of a new chakra in the near future, which will be located between the root chakra and the sacral chakra. This chakra will only appear in the adult human being. It will be especially important during pregnancy.

From the very beginning here on Earth, the unborn child will be able, in the womb of its mother, to absorb the natural male and female cosmic energy through this chakra. This will enable the child to connect not only to the naturalness of the cosmic forces but also to a naturalness of behavior with regard to its inherent masculinity or femininity.

Soon, however, men will also be able to benefit from the development of this chakra. They will be connected to the natural masculine force—to a power that is protective of woman and child, but is also characterized by understanding and love for the members of his family without the assumption of absolute superiority. The traditional father model—that of the ruler over the family—will fall away.

The beginning of the development of this chakra has been planned by the divine intelligence for the year 2024, when the human community will have reached a certain stage of development. This stage is directly related to the development of the crystalline systems in the body of the human being.

Exercise for the Sacral Chakra

Visualize or speak the number sequence 3 7 1 7 three times.
Activate the healing frequencies in your palms.

Then place your hands on your sacral chakra. Breathe deeply and concentrate on your sacral chakra. Through your power of thought, illuminate it with an emerald-green light.

Now prepare to enter into thought contact with your parents. It is of no matter whether your parents are in the physical world or already in the heaven of human beings. Their souls will hear you. It is important for your sacral chakra to purify the relationship with them, the people closest to you.

Now imagine that your mother is standing in front of you. She is looking at you. Send out a beautiful ray of light from your heart to your mother's heart.

The love of your hearts unites you.

And then speak the following words . . .
"I thank you for giving me life. I thank you for the fact that I exist due to you. Forgive me if I ever hurt you in my life.

I forgive you for everything negative that has happened between us. Forgiveness frees us.

I send you love.

Bless you. I love you. Thank you."

Your father is now standing next to your mother.

Your father is looking at you. Send a beautiful ray of light from your heart to your father's heart as well.

And then speak the following words . . .
"I thank you for the fact that I exist due to you. Forgive me if I ever hurt you in my life.

I forgive you for everything negative that has happened between us. Forgiveness frees us.

I send you love.

Bless you. I love you. Thank you."

Now send your parents the gratitude of your heart. Gratitude and the purest essence unite you.

If you have brothers and sisters, send them the love and gratitude of your heart. Forgive them for everything negative that has happened between you. Ask them to forgive you too. Forgiveness sets you free.

The purest essence unites you all. Bless all your brothers and sisters with the love of your heart. Let these pure divine feelings work between you.

Say goodbye to your parents and siblings in your thoughts and let them return to a place they like to be.

Concentrate on your sacral chakra again and unite with its consciousness. Observe what is happening in the world of this chakra and which light beings are present within it.

Now ask the consciousness of your sacral chakra . . .
"Do you have a message for me?
What can I do for your healing?
What can I do for my consciousness development? I receive all information with gratitude. Thank you, thank you, thank you."

Illuminate your sacral chakra with the clear orange light once again and imagine that there is a beautiful, translucent orange crystal within. Send out the love of your heart to it.

Bless it and bless yourself on all levels of your being.

Take your time. If you have received information, write it down.

The Solar Plexus Chakra

The solar plexus is your inner sun and your direct connection to your Higher Self. Your Higher Self is connected with your light companions and your family in the heaven of human beings. It transmits information to you, as well as the love of the light world and its beings. At the same time, it connects you with the information and details of the earthly task you agreed upon, together with your Higher Self, before your arrival on this planet.

Your solar plexus is also the center of the subtle crystalline systems of your body. This network connects you with the crystalline systems in the Earth and with the crystalline systems of this galaxy. It connects you with the light, the love, and the wisdom of the crystals.

Human beings will be communicating with their Higher Self more and more. Through their connection to their Higher Self, human beings will not only be guided during their earthly incarnation particularly well, but through this constant contact with their Higher Self, their intuition will also develop. In earlier times, humankind possessed an intuition that was greater and much more prominent than it is today, but it has been manipulated by the dark forces to such an extent that humankind has lost it almost completely. Some human beings have developed their intuition again through spiritual work, but most move around with no guidance from their Higher Self here on this planet and, consequently, with no intuition. Yet intuition is an indispensable human quality, a precursor to telepathy.

The loss of intuition has caused the whole human community to wander blindly through life and their daily obligations. It blocked human hearts and left human beings to live on this planet with no mental security, because they were no longer able to rely intuitively on anything at all. Due to this loss of intuition, no one could give anyone else good and safe advice with absolute certainty either. And human beings were not even able to find answers within themselves. The separation from oneself and from one's Higher Self has caused not only a personal but also a global disorientation of human civilization.

A blocked solar plexus chakra prevents energy from flowing to the stomach and digestive tract. As a result, the human being is constantly plagued by feelings of fear concerning the loss of life energy and the loss of the ability to absorb nutrition and, consequently, basic life forces as well. This constant subconscious fear of lack and the loss of vitality led and still leads to numerous diseases of the human system.

The negative influence on the solar plexus caused by unprocessed negative relationships that connect a person with other people, beings or human souls is very strong. Unprocessed issues, anger, hatred, defamation and bad thoughts about others create an energetic bond, between the human being and the being or soul concerned, that limits all those involved.

The negative energy around a particular issue determines the relationship to that person and to any other people, beings or souls who stand in precisely this negative relationship to this person. Endless condemnation of others causes a human being to live in the prison of their own emitted thoughts, because through them they are bound to the other person, being or soul. A positive reprogramming of this person liberates and at the same time protects them from negative foreign energies, because dark energies can no longer find anywhere to attach themselves in the system of this now positively thinking person.

Be aware that negative thoughts do not belong to you, because, like every other human being, you are the purest essence of the Divine Source. You carry the purest divine essence within you. Keep reminding yourself of that. Pure thoughts free you from the cycle of negative energetic ties to other people, beings or souls. In this way you find your center and your intuition can develop.

Exercise for the Solar Plexus Chakra

*Visualize or speak the number sequence **3717** three times.*

Activate the healing frequencies in your palms and then place your hands on your solar plexus chakra.

Breathe deeply and concentrate on your solar plexus chakra. Through your power of thought, illuminate it with a radiant golden-yellow light. Your chakra is shining like the sun.

And then speak the following words . . .

"Now and in this space, I connect with my Higher Self. I hereby connect with the guiding information that I have left in the care of my Higher Self. I connect with the frequency of my own intuition.

I raise the frequency of my own intuition with the power of my own will.

My intention is pure and clear."

Breathe deeply, in and out.

And then speak the following words . . .

"Now and in this space, I activate the center of the crystal network in my solar plexus.

In this moment, my solar plexus creates the center of my crystal network and further crystal networks throughout my body.

In this moment, my solar plexus connects with the crystal networks of the Earth and the crystal networks of this galaxy.

In this moment, my solar plexus connects me to the wisdom, information, and energy of the crystal networks of the Earth and the galaxy.

My spiritual consciousness is increased in this moment. Thank you, thank you, thank you."

Breathe deeply. Concentrate again on your solar plexus and connect with its consciousness. Observe what is happening in the world of this chakra and which light beings are present within it.

Now ask the consciousness of your solar plexus chakra . . .

"Do you have a message for me?

What can I do for your healing?

What can I do for my consciousness development? I receive all information with gratitude. Thank you, thank you, thank you."

Illuminate this chakra once again with clear golden-yellow light and imagine that there is a beautiful translucent golden crystal within.

Send out the love of your heart to it.

Bless it and bless yourself on all levels of your being.

Take your time. If you have received information, write it down.

The Heart Chakra

The heart chakra connects you with your heart and with your soul. A complete healing of your heart chakra and your heart brings you an absolute connection to every possibility that the divine world has to offer.

The healing of your heart brings you an absolute connection to the cosmic healing frequencies. Through the optimal functioning of the light chakras above your head, your primal frequencies, your primal information and your primal essence will then flow to you from the Divine Source. The love that flows to you from the Divine Source is the strongest, most powerful, and most loving element that exists.

At this time, it is vital for human beings to remember.

To remember how beautiful and full of light their soul is.

To remember that their divine essence connects them to all that is essential.

This memory brings healing to human beings. It brings them healing and orientation in the earthly world. Through their remembering, human beings lose their fear of the present and also of the future. Through their remembering, they can free themselves from their dark, manipulated past.

With their understanding and remembering, human beings cease to judge other human beings. This liberates them and brings them personal freedom. Personal freedom that is transmitted to other human beings.

With their understanding and remembering, human beings learn to replace their negative emotions and thoughts with positivity. Negative emotions and thoughts prevent the human heart from healing.

Use the number sequence **8 7 8 7** for remembering. This sequence of numbers binds you to the purest essence of humankind, and it connects you to the soul of humanity that desires nothing more than the activation and return of the purity of the human heart.

This number sequence — **8 7 8 7** — also has a beautiful transparent frequency. It is as beautiful as the purest, most translucent crystal. It is important to know that when you begin to work with this sequence of numbers you are activating the presence of the light beings that are connected to this transparent frequency.

These light beings will stay close to you if you so wish. Their light bodies appear angel-like but are transparent, and every part of their bodies looks like made of cut crystals. They also differ from angels in that they do not have light-filled wings. Yet they move with the elegance and grace of angels.

After pronouncing or activating this sequence of numbers, they come close to you and help you connect with the purest essence of humankind. They are light healers of the soul of humanity, which has a similar structure to beautiful cut crystal. Their soul, however, is much more luminous and their frequency so brilliant and sparkling that they are able to connect with the lights of the cosmos and with the lights of other light beings.

Once humanity has healed completely, their light will be even more radiant and luminous.

Exercise for the Heart Chakra

Visualize or speak the number sequence 3 7 1 7 three times.

Activate the healing frequencies in your palms. Then you can place your hands on your heart chakra.

Breathe deeply and concentrate on your heart chakra. Through your power of thought, illuminate it with an emerald-green light. Illuminate your heart.

Unite the light of your heart and your heart chakra and create one great light.

Now, in front of your heart, visualize the sequence of numbers **8 7 8 7**. It is best to visualize it in silver light. Visualize this row of numbers behind your back at the level of your heart in silver light too.

You observe luminous crystal beings coming to be near you, to help you heal your worries and any accumulated negativity. This negativity blocks the energy of your heart. The crystal beings help you to find your way back to your divine purity and divine essence.

Observe how your heart is permeated by the transparent frequencies of the purest essence of humanity. Your cells take up this frequency and release any burdening negativities that have hindered them in their consciousness development.

The cells of your heart release any burdening elements and are healed in the frequency of the purest human divine essence.

And then speak the following words . . .

"Now and in this space, I connect with the consciousness of my heart and with the consciousness of my heart chakra.

Now and in this space, I release everything that is burdensome and that distances me from the purity of my heart. At this very moment, everything negative leaves my heart and heart chakra.

I connect with the frequency of the love of the Divine Source.

The love of the Divine Source now flows through my heart and fills it with the unconditional love of the Divine Source. Gratitude flows through my heart.

Love nourishes me, love heals me.

Love is my essence. Love is my existence.

I am unconditional love."

Now, in front of the number sequence **8 7 8 7** that you have visualized in front of and behind your heart, imagine the sign of infinity, a horizontal eight. By doing this, you ensure that the effect of the number sequence continues and that the frequency of love flows without ceasing to your heart. In this way you support the subsequent healing of your heart.

Concentrate again on your heart chakra and unite with its consciousness. Observe what is happening in the world of this chakra and which light beings are present within it.

Now ask the consciousness of your heart chakra . . .
   "Do you have a message for me?
   What can I do for your healing?
   What can I do for my consciousness development? I receive all information with gratitude. Thank you, thank you, thank you."

Illuminate your heart chakra once again with clear emerald-green light and imagine that there is a beautiful translucent emerald within.
   Send out the love of your heart to it.
   Bless it and bless yourself on all levels of your being.
   Take your time. If you have received information, write it down.

Introduction of the Cosmic Pharmacy through the Number Sequence 8787

For the exercise with your heart chakra we asked you to visualize the number **8 7 8 7** in front of and behind your heart. There was a very important reason for this.

Through this, we have enabled you to connect to the "Cosmic Pharmacy," which contains all the frequencies and subtle substances that the human body, mind, and soul need. This sequence of numbers and the frequency of gratitude give you access to the Cosmic Pharmacy, which we will tell you about in more detail in the following chapters.

By visualizing the number sequence **8 7 8 7** in silver, you also connect to subtle light-filled colloidal silver. For you, that means specifically that your heart can absorb the healing frequency of colloidal silver and heal emotional structures in your heart.

Your cells receive additional help in ridding themselves of burdensome elements.

Your heart distributes the frequency of this subtle colloidal silver throughout your body with the help of your blood circulation. This gives your body the opportunity to rid itself of any inflammatory foci it may still be carrying.

The stress that the human community experiences practically every day causes a wide variety of inflammations and diseases in the human body and weakens the organism's immunity.

Colloidal silver is able to kill a wide variety of microbes and germs within a few minutes. Unlike colloidal silver in physical form, light-filled colloidal silver has no side effects. *All of the frequencies and substances from the Cosmic Pharmacy have their own intelligence and know the dosage necessary at that moment. Accordingly, there is no danger of overdosing.*

Human beings are receiving more and more help from divine intelligence because they are now ready for it. We have told you time and again that human beings would be given further possibilities for healing their physical bodies as well as for developing spiritually. That time is now.

And you have just taken your first steps.

Your first contact with the Cosmic Pharmacy has just taken place.

The Cosmic Pharmacy contains everything that human beings need for healing. The gates to it have just opened.

A pure heart is the key to the gates of the Cosmic Pharmacy!

The Throat Chakra

All relationships are stored in the throat chakra. All stressful relationships limit the function of this chakra. And in contrast, all positive relationships support the good functioning of this chakra.

If you look at the world stored in your throat chakra, you will see that it is mainly your stressful, "ill-fated" relationships – those that you have not yet ended, whether energetically or physically – that are stored there. People who often think about the past are energetically connected to it through the back side of this chakra, in their neck, because this is the part of their body, and also their back, where the past is stored.

People often feel that they are suffocating in certain relationships because these relationships link them to similar relationships in the past. Their throat chakra is therefore often constricted and the light has no power to illuminate the present time and the present relationships. These relationships are then shadowed, as it were; they have no healthy energy in them. Most relationships of this kind fall apart sooner or later.

Another important cause of poor functioning of the throat chakra is the lack of a positive relationship with oneself. Lack of self-love. Lack of self-love destroys all partnerships and interpersonal relationships. A lack of self-love makes people constantly look for faults in others. Lack of self-love leads a person to judge and condemn others. If people are content with themselves and love themselves, they have no reason to attack and judge others. Those who do not love themselves sufficiently are often shown an emblematic mirror from the outside so that they can see what they still have to process within themselves. They themselves have not yet managed to transform what bothers them about others.

Lack of self-love brings unrest into many areas of life. It often also causes illness, because a lack of self-love does not allow a human being to vibrate in the healthy light frequency of love.

When human beings find peace and harmony with themselves, as well as peace and harmony with others, their throat chakra begins to connect to the morphogenetic field of peace, harmony, contentment, and love. Their thyroid gland, which lies in the area of this chakra, can then absorb the frequency of happiness and their body begins to heal. The thyroid gland influences a large number of functions in the human body. It also influences the psyche of the human being, as does the thymus gland, which is able to connect to the rays of the Central Sun after the throat chakra has been healed.

And the entire respiratory system, including the lungs, begins to absorb more oxygen and therefore more life energy, thanks to the increased function of the throat chakra. As a result of the clarity gained in relationships with others and in the relationship with oneself, the throat chakra can radiate and bring sufficient vitality and oxygen into every action of daily life.

Through the healing of relationships, the heart chakra, in which lack of self-love is also encoded, also radiates. It is above all, your mental relationship to your parents that is stored in your throat chakra. Emotional blockages to do with problems concerning parents are primarily stored in your sacral chakra.

Exercise for the Throat Chakra

Visualize or speak the number sequence 3717 three times.

Activate the healing frequencies in your palms. Then place your hands on your throat chakra. Breathe deeply and concentrate on your throat chakra. Through your power of thought, illuminate it with an azure blue light.

Prepare to make peace with other people, beings, and souls that burden you.

Prepare to make peace with yourself. Prepare to understand that one of your greatest tasks here on Earth consists in finding self-love within yourself.

It consists in realizing that, here on this Earth, you are passing through an earthly school of life, in realizing that your understanding of situations you find yourself in will move you forward and improve your ability to love yourself—to love unconditionally.

Loving yourself unconditionally is perhaps one of your greatest tasks in this incarnation.

And then speak the following words . . .

"Now and in this space, I choose to make peace with all those people, beings, and souls who have hurt me.

I connect with the frequencies of peace.

I connect with the angels of peace.

I ask the angels of peace to remove all negative energetic bonds that connect and influence us negatively. My intention is pure and clear.

I ask the angels of peace to help me find love for myself.

I ask the angels of peace to dissolve into light all those situations that prevent me from loving myself.

I make peace with all people, beings, and souls. I make peace with myself. The healing of my throat chakra is happening now and in this space, in all spaces and times of my reality.

Thank you, thank you, thank you."

Breathe deeply and imagine your throat chakra expanding more and more.

Then concentrate again on your throat chakra and connect with its consciousness. Observe what is happening in the world of this chakra and which light beings are present within it.

Now ask the consciousness of your throat chakra . . .

"Do you have a message for me?

What can I do for your healing?

What can I do for my consciousness development? I receive all information with gratitude. Thank you, thank you, thank you."

Imagine the sequence of numbers **8 7 8 7** in a metallic golden color in front of and behind your throat chakra. This sequence of numbers connects you with the Cosmic Pharmacy and with its knowledge. It connects you with the colloidal gold that is within. The metallic golden color is able to neutralize stressful thought patterns that your throat chakra has absorbed. Colloidal gold helps you to open up and activate the energy pathways that run through your body. It brings you vitality and illuminates all the burdensome patterns stored in your system. It regenerates your body, soul, and mind.

Let the healing frequency of this sequence of numbers take effect. Illuminate your heart chakra once again with clear emerald green light and imagine that there is a beautiful translucent emerald within.

Send out the love of your heart to it.

Bless it and bless yourself on all levels of your being.

Take your time. If you have received information, write it down.

The Ear Chakras

The greatest burden that negatively affects the ear chakras is non-forgiveness: not forgiving others, not being forgiven by others and not forgiving yourself.

Many human beings are not aware that, to promote their growth, they have programmed the different situations they meet in their earthly life before their incarnation. But that is exactly how it is. In doing this, individuals often created situations that they later find completely illogical and unnecessary. That is why many human beings constantly reproach themselves for having hurt someone, and suffer from a guilty conscience. They blame themselves for having failed.

Forgive yourself for your past! Make a clean break with your past, separate yourself from it and start again—with a new conscience and with new insights that you wouldn't have if you hadn't gone through certain *situations in the past. Your insights from these situations have allowed you to grow.* Please stop constantly blaming yourself and forgive yourself for your past. If you are caught up in your past the whole time, you are robbing yourself of your own vitality and life force. You can't move forward like that. Your past is holding you back.

With blockages in your ear chakras you deprive yourself of clairaudience. Many people who suffer from ringing in their ears, also called tinnitus, are adversely affected by feelings of guilt and non-forgiveness of themselves. Tinnitus is very common in these times because stress in combination with electrosmog literally blocks your ear chakras and transforms the original subtle vibration of these chakras into high frequency, unbearable vibrations.

In these times, human beings are unable to listen to the surrounding world and are unable to listen to themselves, to their soul, and their heart. With each new incarnation on Earth they have lost their clairaudience even more. The blockages are too strong. Great burdens, stress, and manipulation by the dark forces have brought human beings to a state where they have ceased to connect through their ear chakras to the cosmic language and to the language of the beings of light who are always close to human beings.

Due to manipulation by the dark forces, human beings have cut themselves off from the possibility of communication with the light world. This was one of the countless dark plans devised to disconnect humankind from their light-filled environment and to push them into isolation. Human beings have thereby also disconnected themselves from communication with animals, plants, and minerals, and from communication with water, air, fire, and earth—all the elements of nature.

Another major negative influence on the ear chakras is a frequency that is emitted through the audio tracks of the media. This frequency acts like a constant harmful background noise. It mainly attacks the ear chakras, it penetrates your aura, causing gaps to form in it, so it is then easy for it to penetrate into further areas of the human system through other frequencies. If you are using telecommunication devices, you are permanently exposed to low-frequency waves that generate fear in human beings—and also aggression and hatred—with the result that they become more and more isolated from their environment. Yet the human being has been created for a life in the collective. And all human beings have been provided by divine intelligence with all they need for clairaudience.

Through the activation and correct functioning of your ear chakras you will be able to communicate not only with the surrounding light world and light beings once more, but also with the animals you love.

And after renewing communication with the animal kingdom, human beings will no longer even consider eating animal beings, all of which bear consciousness and feelings within them—but which human beings have heard nothing of, so far.

You will be able to communicate with every stone and crystal that humankind has hitherto considered inanimate, dead; with every object, because every object also has its own consciousness; and you will understand that every being and every object has a consciousness with which you can communicate.

You will notice that the world around you expands greatly, because it is now possible for you to communicate with even the smallest plant—and this plant will tell you about everything that moves it and what it has experienced.

You will find that your steps forward in life will bring you much more joy, simply because you will perceive much more in the way of vibrant happenings around you.

You will become more perceptive.

Exercise for the Ear Chakras

Visualize or speak the number sequence 3717 three times.
Activate the healing frequencies in your palms. Then place your hands on your ear chakras. Breathe deeply and concentrate on your ear chakras. Through your power of thought, illuminate them with pink light. This color is the color of forgiveness.

Prepare to perform a ritual of forgiveness out of the deepest and purest intention.
Now speak the sequence of numbers 35791 three times.
In this way you open the dimensions, times, and spaces in which forgiving is necessary. Forgiving other people, beings, and souls. Being forgiven yourself by other people, beings, and souls.
And forgiving yourself.
The light world enables you to open up these dimensions so that every person, soul, and being really hears you.

And then speak the following words . . .
"With this number sequence, I open all dimensions, spaces, and times in which forgiving is necessary on all levels of my life and on all levels of my being.
I ask all those beings of light who can help me to connect me now and in this space with the consciousness of all people, beings, and souls who are still waiting for me to forgive them.

With all my heart I forgive every person, being, and soul.

I now ask to be connected with the consciousness of all people, beings, and souls who have not yet forgiven me. Please give me your heartfelt forgiveness.

I now ask my soul to forgive me for having brought it into situations in which it was hurt by my behavior.

I forgive myself for harming myself. I forgive myself for having had to constantly suffer from my behavior in the past.

I understand that my past has been programmed in detail by my soul and my Higher Self."

Now imagine that near your ear chakras there are golden signs of infinity, horizontal eights. Visualize how these healing signs rotate in all directions and how the subtle energetic connections that have linked you to the negativities of other people, beings or souls are transformed into light by the light and speed of these horizontal eights.

Now ask Archangel Michael to purify all the remaining negativities that still exist between you and other people, beings, and souls.

Now ask Archangel Raphael, who regenerates everything and brings it into harmony, to heal the relationships between you and other people, beings, and souls.

And then speak the following words . . .

"Now and in this space, I release myself from my dark past.

I bless my past.

I bless all people, beings, and souls who have hurt me.

I connect through this with the frequency of my clairaudience.

Now and in this space, I activate my clairaudience.

I am absolutely connected with the cosmic language of light.

I now fix my state of healing with the number sequence: *35791. 35791. 35791.*

Thank you, thank you, thank you."

Concentrate again on your ear chakras and connect with their consciousness. Observe what is happening in the world of these chakras and which light beings are present within them.

Now ask the consciousness of your ear chakras . . .

"Do you have a message for me?

What can I do for your healing?

What can I do for my consciousness development? I receive all information with gratitude. Thank you, thank you, thank you."

Illuminate your ear chakras once again with clear pink light and imagine that there are beautiful translucent pink crystals within them.

Send out the love of your heart to them.

Bless them and bless yourself on all levels of your being.

Take your time. If you have received information, write it down.

The Third Eye

Every human being who develops spiritually or is concerned with spirituality desires clairvoyance. In ancient times clairvoyance was an innate ability—up until the time when humanity began to be manipulated by the dark beings. Clairvoyant abilities are now being given back to humankind.

Human beings who have been meditating for a long time have probably already reactivated their clairvoyant abilities. Some human beings brought their abilities with them to this planet at birth. The chakra of their third eye was already open before their arrival on Earth.

Many children who are incarnating on planet Earth at this time, and many children who will incarnate on planet Earth, have the ability to communicate and see with their third eye from birth. Through the power of their innate ability, they will connect to the cosmic knowledge and information coming from the Divine Source. Many children of these and future times will also participate in the "cosmic teaching" of consciousness development. They will be able to connect to the morphogenetic fields of the cosmic school in which billions of extraterrestrial beings are participating.

This teaching will lead them to the truth and to information about the complexity of the universe.

The education that currently takes place on planet Earth is outdated and highly flawed. In your schools, children learn about historical events that in some cases happened differently or did not happen at all. The present education that human children receive gives them only a small percentage of the knowledge for life that they should receive. The development of telepathy and intuition was taken from human children in particular by the dark forces. But the new generation of children is coming and they will arrive on the planet with different abilities and, through their accumulated knowledge, broaden the horizons of people who will not be able to use their third eye in this lifetime.

Many human beings who have experienced the atrocities of the past have suppressed their abilities, or have lost the strength to use their innate clairvoyant abilities at all. But they too can reactivate their third eye. To do this we gave you a short affirmation for neutralizing your personal oaths in our earlier messages (see here in Bonus Affirmations at the end of the book, page 187).

The following exercise is for activating your third eye.

Exercise for the Third Eye Chakra

*Visualize or speak the number sequence **3717** three times.*

Then activate the healing frequencies in your palms.

If you wish, you can place a purple amethyst on your third eye chakra. Amethyst purifies this chakra and transforms accumulated blockages in its crystal networks.

If you have no crystal at hand, you can simply imagine it.

Breathe deeply and place or visualize the purple amethyst on your third eye. A beautiful, radiant crystal.

Connect with its consciousness and ask it to help you purify your third eye chakra. Imagine that through this crystal a beautiful, purple-silver ray of light reaches your third eye.

This ray of light has the ability to transform; and it transforms with its light and through the power of its radiation all the accumulated blockages and thought patterns that burden this chakra.

Now let this ray of light pass through your pineal gland—your epiphysis—which is located between your cerebral hemispheres.

This purple-silver ray of light coming from divine intelligence connects your third eye with your pineal gland in your brain.

Your third eye and your pineal gland shine beautifully.

And then speak the following words . . .

"Now and in this space, I hand over to divine intelligence all the blockages and burdens that contaminate the chakra of my third eye and my pineal gland. Now and in this space, all these blockages and burdens dissolve in the purple-silver light of divine transformation, in all the times and spaces of my whole existence.

With all my heart, I forgive all people, beings, and souls who have hurt me, in all the times and spaces of my whole existence.

Now and in this space, I ask for the forgiveness of every person, being, and soul I have harmed. I ask for forgiveness in all the times and spaces of our whole existence.

Now and in this space, I forgive myself for having harmed myself through my behavior. I forgive myself in all the times and spaces of my whole existence.

My intention is pure and clear.

Thank you, thank you, thank you."

Now, in your mind go to the chakra of your third eye. Imagine that there is a three-dimensional flower of life in this chakra. This symbol is also purple-silver in color.

The whole amethyst connects with the symbol of the flower of life.

The flower of life is a two-dimensional representation of a multidimensional structure. It brings you harmonization and an additional purification of your third eye.

The flower of life brings you into connection with the divine order and its structure.

Concentrate again on your third eye and connect with its consciousness. Observe what is happening in the world of this chakra and which light beings are present within it.

Now ask the consciousness of the chakra of the third eye . . .

"Do you have a message for me?

What can I do for your healing?

What can I do for my consciousness development? I receive all information with gratitude. Thank you, thank you, thank you."

Illuminate the chakra of your third eye with clear purple light once again and imagine that there is a beautiful, translucent, dark blue crystal within.

Send out the love of your heart to it.

Bless it and bless yourself on all levels of your being.

Take your time. If you have received information, write it down.

The Crown Chakra

The crown chakra is a "receiver" for energy flowing in from the cosmos. The more subtle human beings become, the more able they are to absorb the subtle frequencies and information of their environment. They then begin to masterfully recode the morphogenetic fields that are around them and use the information contained in these fields for positive purposes.

Subtlety is typical of the Golden Age and teaches humankind to adapt to their earthly as well as cosmic environment.

The subtle information that reaches human beings connects them to morphogenetic fields of the most varied kinds. This gives human beings the possibility to connect, with pure intention, to the morphogenetic field of healing knowledge, for example, or to the field of the healers themselves. They can connect to the field of doctors or natural medicine. They can also connect to the field of different languages or realms created by humanity or other civilizations.

This subtle information reaches the human brain, whose synapses also become more subtle. A human being who regularly connects to cosmic energy has a greater number of active synapses that can recode the information of the morphogenetic fields. The light impulses that arise in the brain through this activity attract subtle light information.

Through the repeated connection to cosmic energy and its information, the capacity of the human brain constantly increases. In many people, brain capacity has already increased from about 6 percent to 20 or even 30 percent. That is a huge evolutionary leap, because until now it has not been possible for human beings to expand their brain capacity. Since the influx of the subtle light frequencies that began arriving on the planet in 2020, the evolutionary development of the human being has been enormous.

Life energy flows particularly through the crown chakra to the human being. The human heart absorbs it into its interior and works with it in the form of the heartbeat. At regular intervals, the heart transmits the cosmic energy entering through the crown chakra to the heart chakra, while at the same time receiving the energy of the Earth and absorbing it into its muscular tissues. The crown chakra also absorbs the energy of the sun's rays and passes it on to the whole body. Spending time in nature always strengthens the work of both chakras.

The cosmic energy flowing toward human beings includes the entire energetic spectrum: every color, form, tone, and frequency. These and other cosmic components interact and are given to the human being in a "package"—cosmic life energy.

Without realizing it, human beings are in constant communication with cosmic intelligence, which gives them their life energy in the form of these colors, shapes, sounds, and frequencies.

In this way, cosmic intelligence speaks to the consciousness of the human body. But the consciousness of the human body not only communicates with these cosmic components but also with the earthly components in its environment, which the human body needs for its existence on this planet. Communication with the environment and its frequencies happens automatically, without the human mind and soul registering it.

Your body also has its own language. It is connected to the morphogenetic fields of knowledge about the human body and of knowledge about the physical material of human beings. If the crown chakra is working well, it facilitates communication with the environment and the connection to certain morphogenetic fields.

Thank your body for its work with the cosmic life energy and bless it for all it does for you. Bless its intelligence.

Exercise for the Crown Chakra

Visualize or speak the number sequence 3 7 1 7 three times.

Activate the healing frequencies in your palms and then place your hands on your crown chakra. Breathe deeply.

Now imagine that a beautiful light in all the colors of the rainbow is flowing to your crown chakra. Your crown chakra is so active that it forms a light-filled funnel enabling it to absorb as much of this cosmic energy as possible.

Breathe deeply through your mouth and let the oxygen spread throughout your body. Imagine how the oxygen is penetrating all your organs, your arms and legs.

Now breathe deeply through your nose. Fill all the chambers of your head with oxygen. Breathing deeply through your nose stimulates all the neural pathways and synapses in your brain. Feel how the oxygen refreshes you.

Now breathe alternately through your mouth and your nose.

Through your breathing you also distribute the light-filled rainbow energy throughout your body and your head.

All the chakras of your body radiate beautifully.

All the chakras of your head radiate.

See how your whole body radiates. Your spine radiates this rainbow light.

Through your crown chakra, this rainbow light continuously enters and enlivens your body. The consciousness and intelligence of your body merge with this magical rainbow light and absorb the healing effects of this wonderful light into your heart.

Your heart receives all its colors, shapes, sounds, and frequencies. You feel how your heart and your body are receiving more and more cosmic life energy. Your heart beats regularly.

Visualize above your crown chakra the sign of infinity. In this way, you ensure that this cosmic life energy will continue to flow to you.

Concentrate again on your crown chakra and connect with its consciousness. Observe what is happening in the world of this chakra and which light beings are present within it.

Now ask the consciousness of your crown chakra . . .
"Do you have a message for me?

What can I do for your healing?

What can I do for my consciousness development?

I receive all information with gratitude. Thank you, thank you, thank you."

Illuminate your crown chakra with the clear rainbow-colored light once again and imagine that there is a beautiful, translucent lilac-violet crystal within.

Send out the love of your heart to it.

Bless it and bless yourself on all levels of your being.

Take your time. If you have received information, write it down.

The Light Chakras above Your Head

The five light-filled chakras above your head are also receivers of information and frequencies that reach you from the divine intelligence of the Central Source. They form a kind of "antenna." The number of light chakras depends on the spiritual development of the person. Five light chakras form the basis and, as you develop spiritually, more chakras appear.

These chakras receive primal information and primal frequencies that help you in your spiritual development as well as in the light-filled development of your body.

Since the beginning of 2019, an increasing amount of this primal information and these primal frequencies has been arriving on planet Earth—even more intensively since Easter 2020—and they are healing the entire planet and its citizens, its plants and animals. Its plants and animals have begun to connect incredibly quickly to their primal information and primal frequencies, and they have also now begun to regenerate much more easily.

Mother Earth is also beginning to connect and is reassuming her original power with more and more ease.

Moreover, an increasing amount of primal information and primal frequencies is returning to human beings, and the flow of impulses and light information, transmitted to human beings through their life energy for the regeneration of their DNA, is intensifying. Around Easter 2020, the energetic overwriting of human DNA strands intensified. This information also follows the path through the light chakras, and is encoded into these chakras in a certain form and in accordance with the needs of each individual person.

The light chakras work best when the human being's heart is pure and free from selfish, manipulative, and negative patterns, thoughts, and emotions of any kind. When the human heart is purified and pristine, the individual light chakras expand to a considerable size, enabling them to receive the light information that comes from divine intelligence.

This light information connects you with your divine essence, which is held in the divine Central Source. It enables you to grow in consciousness and reminds you that each one of you is your own creator. Each one of you carries a part of this divine home within you and each one of you is able to receive the divine light information and light frequencies.

Your pure heart makes this possible for you.

A certain proportion of the cells that are found in the human heart have already connected you with the divine intelligence and with your divine home.

Do you remember that we spoke of certain regions in the heart, of certain cells that have already increased their light vibration? Through this you were able to form a light-filled connection with your divine home. These cells are located in the depths of your heart, in what is called the "sacred" chamber, which I am sure many of you have heard about. Mystics from all cultures have told you of this and it has also been written about. This chamber is the most energetically significant place in your heart.

Although this place inside your heart—near the sinus node—is tiny, there is a whole universe within. This chamber is the entrance, exit, and passageway to the field of the Divine Source and to the fields of consciousness of your personality. This tiny place in your heart is the entrance, exit, and passageway to all the information and frequencies of the Divine Source. This tiny place connects you with your divine home and with the essence of God.

Those of you who have mastered the gift of visualization and can travel effortlessly into the depths of your heart can very quickly find yourselves in the realm of infinity of the Divine Source. You can find yourself in the realm of the zero-point field, which offers possibilities for all possible possibilities!

This chamber in the depths of your heart is activated by the purity of your thoughts and by the frequency of gratitude. The frequency of gratitude opens the gates to this sacred chamber, tiny in size but grand in its essence, vast and infinite like the universe itself.

The frequency of gratitude opens the doors to the sacred chamber in your heart. And when your thought fields are purified, this chamber and access to the Divine Source are activated automatically. That is where the key that we have always talked about is to be found. The key you carry in your heart.

This chamber is a gateway that remains open at all times if you do not poison your thoughts and if thoughts that have possibly been poisoned do not infect your heart.

When this sacred chamber is activated, the first ray of divine light flashes out in the human being. This ray connects the human being with further rays of the divine world and with divine information. This divine information is in turn identical to the innate information of the human being concerned, because every human being originated from the Divine Source. Every human being and every soul.

The first ray of light that flashes out in the heart of a human being causes them to remember their perfect being. The first ray connects this human being with their primal information and primal frequencies. The first ray that penetrates the sacred chamber of the human being is accompanied by divine beings of light who take care that the heart chamber does not close again. With this first ray, the human being is allocated a whole group of light beings who have a great divine task. And that is—to remind the human being again and again of their essence, of their knowledge, their consciousness and their origin.

Through the activation of the sacred divine chamber in their heart, the human being is connected to an infinite number of frequencies, lights, colors, sounds, and forms that the heart can decipher and transform into information that the human mind, body, and soul can absorb.

This tiny little chamber in the heart is the absolute key to healing and regeneration and to increasing the spirituality of the human being. This tiny little chamber is a direct gateway to God. This tiny little chamber is a direct gateway to the light world and at the same time a gateway to yourself.

After activation and after the entry of the first divine ray, the physical material of the human being begins to heal, the consciousness of the body increases and the human being begins to vibrate in a higher light-filled frequency. The soul and mind also wish to rid themselves of the last burdens they may still carry. That is why, in many cases, people who have already purified their present incarnation, their mind, and their emotions, are faced with issues from past incarnations that have, as it were, pushed themselves forward in this person's system into a position where they can no longer be ignored. They are shown situations and issues that are foreign to them and in which they see no sense. In this case, it is good to accept these karmic issues with gratitude and to process them with gratitude so that these experiences from the past can also depart and not prevent further light-filled divine rays from penetrating the heart of the human being. The more rays of light that penetrate the human heart, the more divine information, frequencies, sounds, forms, colors, and beings of light are present in the human being.

Through a pure heart, human beings have access to higher dimensions. And also to lower dimensions, if this is necessary in order to purify something there.

Through a pure heart, human beings can move in several dimensions of consciousness at the same time. The third eye chakra allows them to perceive all the individual dimensions and worlds, and the light chakras above their head connect them with these different dimensions and worlds.

These light chakras are subtle gateways to the individual human being's dimensions, spaces, and times. They provide us with energetically coded information that we have collected in the most diverse spaces of our reality. And they are directly connected to the consciousness of our Higher Self. You can connect with your Higher Self through your solar plexus.

The experiences of the soul and mind of a human being— gathered while moving in different worlds without their physical body—are also stored in the memory of the light chakras. Here, experiences in dreams are stored as well. In dreams, the soul and mind of a human being move in the different spaces and times of their non-physical existence. The light chakras sometimes connect the soul with other human souls with whom it meets during sleep.

Moreover, the timelines of human beings are encoded in the light chakras. Through working on your light chakras, it is therefore possible to influence your own life timeline, at least to a certain extent. And there are also worlds of light in the light chakras, just as there are in all the other chakras. Situations encountered and the experiences of a human being are encoded in the light chakras. The only difference is that they are experiences lived outside the physical body.

If a human being experiences energetic manipulation—caused by the transmission of energetic implants, curses or accusations, for example—the light chakras contract and no longer receive information from the Divine Source. A human being who is disabled by energetic implants, for example, and thereby loses energy and strength for the future, needs to be aware of this fact. If human beings wish to free themselves, they must be aware that they are energetically and mentally influenced and that they can free themselves in particular through the power of their will, through forgiveness, perseverance, and their understanding of the situation. They must understand that they will only be able to reconnect to the Divine Source after the implants have been removed. Until then, of course, they will be disconnected from the Divine Source. They must rise above this fact and begin to act. The connection will then be re-established.

In the future, these light chakras will take on an increasingly important task and role in the human being. Through the strong influx of cosmic light and cosmic information, more light chakras will begin to form. They are a gateway to parallel worlds. They are portals that connect human beings with cosmic light and with all their information. Their most important role is to form a connection between the human being and the information of the Divine Source.

Exercise for the Light Chakras above the Head

*Visualize or speak the number sequence **3717** three times.*

Activate the healing frequencies in your palms and then place your hands on your crown chakra. Breathe deeply.

Now imagine that a beautiful light in all the colors of the rainbow is flowing to your crown chakra. Your crown chakra is so active that it forms a light-filled funnel enabling it to absorb as much of this cosmic energy as possible.

Breathe deeply through your mouth and let the oxygen spread throughout your body. Imagine how the oxygen is penetrating all your organs, your arms and legs.

Now breathe deeply through your nose. Fill all the chambers of your head with oxygen. Breathing deeply through your nose stimulates all the neural pathways and synapses in your brain. Feel how the oxygen refreshes you.

Now breathe alternately through your mouth and your nose.

Through your breathing you also distribute the light-filled rainbow energy throughout your body and your head.

All the chakras of your body radiate beautifully.

All the chakras of your head radiate.

Connect mentally with the sacred chamber in your heart.

Tune in to the cosmic frequency of gratitude. A beautiful golden, pink-white color flows into your heart.

Your whole heart takes up this frequency, especially the sacred chamber in your heart, which is a gateway to the Divine Source.

And then speak the following words . . .

"Now and in this space, I activate the sacred chamber in my heart through the power of the frequency of gratitude. Gratitude connects me absolutely with the Divine Source and its love.

I now ask my light chakras to transmit the information received from divine intelligence to the area around the sacred place in my heart.

The sacred chamber in my heart is activated. It receives the information from my light chakras and passes it on to the system of my body, soul, and mind.

My heart is connected with the Divine Source and with its love. The love of the Divine Source regenerates my body and causes the consciousness of my soul and mind to grow. My body, my soul, and my mind absorb all the divine information.

I am connected to the frequency of gratitude. I feel gratitude. I am gratitude.

Thank you, thank you, thank you."

Breathe deeply. Concentrate again on your light chakras and connect with their consciousness. Observe what is happening in the world of these chakras and which light beings are present within them.

Now ask the consciousness of your light chakras . . .

"Do you have a message for me?

What can I do for your healing?

What can I do for my consciousness development? I receive all information with gratitude. Thank you, thank you, thank you."

Illuminate your light chakras once again with golden light and imagine that there are beautiful translucent crystals within them.

Send out the love of your heart to it.

Bless them and bless yourself on all levels of your being.

Take your time. If you have received information, write it down.

A Quick Purification of All Your Chakras and the Securing of This Purification on the Energy Level

You can do the following exercise in the evening before going to bed to help your chakras shine their light, if you have accumulated any negative burdens during the day. Of course, you can also do it as a preventive measure at any other time of day. Your chakras absorb your regular energetic impulses and the light of your thoughts and encode them internally.

For easier visualization, use a metallic golden color when purifying all your chakras. This color helps to reprogram mental burdens that are stuck in your chakras. It is also the color of the future of humanity and the future of the Golden Age.

And this is the exercise . . .

Breathe deeply.

Imagine that the light chakras under your feet are shining beautifully in a metallic golden color. The light chakras under your feet transmit this wonderful, metallic golden light to your root chakra.

Your root chakra transmits this light to the sacral chakra.

From the sacral chakra this light rises to your solar plexus chakra, then to your heart chakra, to your throat chakra, to your ear chakras, to your third eye chakra, to your crown—and the light rises further to the light chakras above your head.

All your chakras are shining beautifully and are filled with the light of the Divine Source.

Now imagine the sign of infinity under your light chakras in the Earth. Then imagine it in the area of your root chakra.

Then in front of your sacral chakra and behind the back of your sacral chakra, in your back.

Then in front of and behind your solar plexus, in the back, in front of and behind your heart chakra, in front of and behind your throat chakra, next to your left and right ear, in front of your third eye chakra, above your crown chakra, and above the light chakras located above your head.

77

And now say in your mind or out loud . . .
"All my chakras are illuminated and activated.
The healing divine light heals all my chakras.
I am connected with the frequency of cosmic healing.
I bless myself on all levels of my being.
I secure the absolute vitality of my chakras,
in this time and in this space.
Thank you, thank you, thank you."

Understanding the significance and role of the chakras is of great importance for you. Cosmic as well as earthly energy can flow to you through your chakras. Your heart absorbs all the incoming information and filters it, even when the information is flowing to the individual chakras and being encoded within them. Your heart is a receiver of all information. It encodes the incoming information to its advantage or disadvantage.

It is no wonder that a person who suffers from constant worry, no matter what kind, will have pain in their physical heart. A person who is permanently under pressure, no matter what kind, suffers from a weighted heart.

Many people who are caught in their thoughts and worries suffer cardiac arrest.

We call it a heart attack. With their constant worries, doubts or other pressures, people prevent their heart from accessing the divine, cosmic energy and love that regulates everything. Divine energy and love guides every living being on this planet, it guides every element on this planet. The course of development is such that everything moves toward the love of the Divine Source.

Human beings who have closed their hearts to divine love have also closed their gateway to themselves. The divine energies that nourish them have no way of penetrating to the divine essence in their soul.

Each chakra has its own vibration and encodes corresponding information within itself. Nevertheless, the entire complex system of the human being is attuned to the vibration and love of the Divine Source.

Your chakras play a big role in your development. The more you purify your chakras, the bigger, more diverse and more beautiful the worlds in your chakras will become and the stronger and more stable will be your connection to the light beings who are responsible for the worlds of your chakras.

The stronger your connection to the light beings in the worlds of your chakras, the more stable your physical sheath will be. And your physical sheath will be able to regenerate thanks to the light of the chakras and start its first light body processes.

Peace with you, peace with us!

5

The Cosmic Pharmacy
Is Open to Humankind!

We have told you many times, dear messengers of light, that reading these texts raises your consciousness. And we can see that you, working with these texts, have already raised your light frequency just by reading them. The words in these texts are positively charged and certain individual words are keys to your healing. Your soul can recode these word keys, and with this recoding the healing process starts. Many of you may be very tired or sleepy, especially when you begin reading. This is because the healing process has begun and your system is releasing the accumulated negativities.

And therefore we are convinced that all of you, dear readers of our texts, have already raised your consciousness and therefore have easier access to the Cosmic Pharmacy of the human community.

∽

Now we would like to talk about the Cosmic Pharmacy in more detail and facilitate your access to it.

The Cosmic Pharmacy, which has an almost infinite field of knowledge, is a pharmacy intended for the human community. Every extraterrestrial civilization has its morphogenetic fields and every civilization has access to its own Cosmic Pharmacy from its respective level of consciousness.

At this very time, the human community has gained access to its own pharmacy!

The morphogenetic fields of the Cosmic Pharmacy were created by divine intelligence at the beginning of the physical existence of humankind. The Cosmic Pharmacy has been used by many generations before you, but that was in the times of Lemuria and Atlantis. After the fall of Atlantis, the human community lost their connection to divine intelligence and thereby their access to this pharmacy.

At this time of your human awakening and development of consciousness, which for humankind is therefore also a time of increasing light frequencies and light vibrations, human beings have again received access to natural remedies and natural preparations that are appropriate for them. For their body and for their soul and mind.

Humanity's access to the natural remedies of this pharmacy is supported by the increased vibrations of the Earth.

The best way to access the Cosmic Pharmacy is through your heart. Your heart, as we have often written, is the key to your information and to your frequencies. Those of you who have succeeded in activating the sacred chamber in your heart and have been able to receive your first rays of divine intelligence have easier access to the remedies of the Cosmic Pharmacy.

All the natural essences and natural remedies that human beings need for their healing are present in this pharmacy.

*The activation of these potentially infinite resources is brought about through your heart with the help of the frequency of gratitude and the number sequence **8787**.*

This number sequence is a number sequence for the healing of human beings. For finding their purest essence. This number sequence connects the human being with the soul of humanity. And the soul of humanity is connected with all the necessary morphogenetic fields that humanity has produced, and with all the morphogenetic fields that have been made available to humanity by divine intelligence.

*The number sequence **8787** connects you with all the resources in the Cosmic Pharmacy that you need. It connects you with all vitamins,* *minerals, amino acids, herbs, plant extracts, trees, essences, aromas, natural hormones, colloidal metals . . . with everything that the human body, the human mind, and the human soul need for their development and healing. At the same time, it connects you with all the frequencies, tones, colors, and geometrical forms that you may need at any given moment.*

The genius of divine intelligence is so wonderful! As already mentioned, morphogenetic fields, which contain the elements appropriate for the respective civilization, were created by divine intelligence for each civilization. Each civilization has access to its own fields. *The development of consciousness is the access key.*

The ingeniously conceived information contained in these fields connects with morphogenetic fields of cosmic frequencies that are picked up by the human heart and encoded there.

The infinite possibilities for the interconnection of the morphogenetic fields, which proceeds at a speed higher than the speed of light, enable the remedies of the Cosmic Pharmacy to reach the human being instantaneously. As soon as you form the intention to connect with the Cosmic Pharmacy and its remedies, the reaction is instantaneous—the human being receives these remedies at the speed of thought.

Individual fields and frequencies, responsible for a certain remedy that a person has just asked for, are connected as one at the moment of intention and can be given immediately.

In the divine world there are no borders or speed limits. There, time does not exist or is of no consequence, and space is movable and flexible.

The intention and the thought of that intention instantly connect the person with the required remedy from the Cosmic Pharmacy.

Another indescribably wonderful feature of this pharmacy is that it is not possible to "overdose" on the administered drug or preparation. The remedies and preparations given to human beings by the Cosmic Pharmacy carry an intelligence of their own. They only enter the human system if the human being needs this remedy. And if a certain element is already present in their system or does not resonate in the human being's system at that moment, it does not enter their system at all. The remedies of the Cosmic Pharmacy are able to give the required dosage themselves. The intelligence of these preparations is divine, for their origin is in the Divine Source.

Again and again we are fascinated by the intelligence of the Divine Source and filled with the greatest admiration for how the divine cosmic world is structured. We are delighted that the opportunity to develop in all directions is given for every situation and for every entity in this infinite happening!

Not even we imagined there to be such an infinite number of possibilities. The increase in our consciousness development is incessant, and at the same rate we are receiving information that is becoming more and more detailed, becoming more extensive and deeper—not only for us, but also for other civilizations.

Not even we ever imagined that there is an answer and a solution for everything as long as we seek the answers with a pure heart. A pure heart has given us infinite possibilities and we would like to pass these possibilities on to you and communicate them to you.

We wish to assist you in finding your essence and in finding the knowledge that has been taken from humanity by the dark forces.

The time has finally come, after millennia, for humankind to return to their knowledge, to their wisdom, and to their possibilities. They are returning to the spiritual stage of their original state.

And we are very happy that we can accompany you and that we can help you with our information.

Peace with you, peace with us!
Yours, Orella

6

Light-Filled Colloidal Metals
and the Task of Physical Gold
with Regard to Human Beings
and the Planet Earth

We would like to share with you some more information about the colloidal metals contained in the Cosmic Pharmacy. Colloidal metals energize and revitalize your body through cosmic, life-giving energy. Your body absorbs this primarily through its energy pathways—meridians, which also run along the surface of your physical body and form part of your geometric matrix. Your geometric matrix is being enlivened and aligned with the matrix of your galaxy and the matrix of your Earth.

Colloidal metals present in the Cosmic Pharmacy are able to greatly energize, nourish, and rejuvenate your body.

Many extraterrestrial civilizations use these cosmic products and revitalize their bodies with the life-giving properties of colloidal metals. Colloidal gold is the "favorite" among the metals. Not only can it heal and rejuvenate all parts of your body, it also penetrates the structures of the DNA, where it causes positive genetic changes. It screens and strengthens telomeres so that certain parts of the chromosomes no longer pass on information concerning aging to the human being.

Human beings can also use colloidal gold to connect to the cosmic Christ energy, which carries an overwhelming energy of love. You know that love nourishes and heals everything you can imagine. The frequency of love is the most powerful of all frequencies. And colloidal gold helps you to connect with this love if you are still experiencing certain problems with the connection.

Gold and the color of gold are a symbol for the infinite flow of light and power in the cosmos. The extraterrestrial civilizations that think and act negatively and have been occupying planet Earth for thousands of years were looking for gold when they arrived and are still looking for it. They extract it from inside the Earth. From these resources they create monoatomic gold. This gold is chemically processed and forms even smaller, more subtle physical particles than colloidal gold.

The dark extraterrestrial civilizations need gold in this form for their regeneration and for its rejuvenating effects. They are unable to connect to the frequency of the light-filled colloidal metals because their heart is closed as a result of manipulative thoughts, malicious intentions, and aggression. That is why they need gold in this physical form. The truth is that they live for several thousand years thanks to this golden substance, because their genetic information is programmed through the properties of gold for longevity.

Extraterrestrial civilizations occupy the planet primarily because there is gold in the Earth. They originally enslaved humanity, under the premise of gaining wealth, power, and domination over all other races in order, with their help, to obtain the raw material that is also so precious to them.

You human beings can work with gold differently. You can use it in physical form as colloidal gold. You can raise your life energy with it, and it regenerates your body. But you can also visualize it. Then it protects you against negative influences from the environment, from energies and negative beings.

You can also use it in the form of light frequencies. You can use it in the form of tones because tones permeate every cell of your body.

The effects of gold were known to the alchemists of times long past. They were punished for their skills in handling gold, but their knowledge is still stored in their common morphogenetic fields. The effects of gold are absolutely fantastic. It is an omnipotent natural remedy that the pharmaceutical system deliberately pushed into the background. The pharmaceutical system knew very well that almost all human diseases could be cured with the frequencies and properties of gold.

The thoughts of human beings can also be healed with golden frequencies. The metallic golden color is the best color for reprogramming or rewriting burdensome thought patterns.

The world and humanity are now striving toward the Golden Age, when the Earth will finally connect with the golden frequencies and rays of cosmic Christ love. The color of gold activates a new energetic form for the new frequencies of the Golden Age in the human heart.

Humanity has suffered too many strong energetic injuries to their systems of body, mind, and soul.

It goes back a long way and is ongoing. The remedies and colloidal metals of the Cosmic Pharmacy are now, at the beginning of the Golden Age, able to bring balance and healing back to human beings.

Human beings who are not yet ready to use the remedies of the Cosmic Pharmacy in light form can use natural remedies and preparations in physical form. Many people need an increased dosage of vital substances, because the material of the physical in particular consumes more vitamins, minerals, and nutrients due to the increased frequencies and energies of the Earth and the cosmos. If you wish, you can combine the use of physical remedies with the remedies of the Cosmic Pharmacy.

The remedies of the Cosmic Pharmacy are of course completely pure and contain none of the additives found in most physically produced preparations. They also have no side effects at all, because they have their own intelligence.

And the best thing is: each and every one of you has access to the Cosmic Pharmacy! It depends solely on the frequency of gratitude that you carry in your heart. That is what connects you with the Cosmic Pharmacy.

And contrary to what most people say, you don't have to worry that gold as a resource is limited. Of course, over millennia, vast quantities of gold and precious metals have already been dug out from the depths of your Earth. But fortunately, your planet has the wonderful ability to regenerate itself, creating more and more of its minerals and precious ores. It creates gold because within the planet this mineral fulfills an important task and function. It forms a system of meridians within. These meridians network the entire planet on the energy level. At the same time, they connect it with the meridians of the galaxy.

The injuries inflicted on the Earth by the extraction of gold are currently "healing" because the Earth is absorbing golden frequencies coming from the cosmos, from the Divine Source. Thanks to these golden energetic frequencies, she can create subtle energetic networks and connect them with the physical gold meridians so that, for the time being, her meridian system is whole, without flaws. The crystal networks in the Earth help with this on the energy level.

By the years 2030 to 2032, humanity should have ascended to the peak of the Golden Age. By then, humanity's consciousness should have developed to the point where it can return its stores of gold, which were used as a means of payment, to the Earth.

During this time, any form of payment will definitely disappear. With the help of technologies that have long been waiting to be used, humanity will then be able to materialize objects. And the supplies of physical gold that have been taken from the planet will then be returned by humanity to the core of the Earth. The Earth will receive them with gratitude and through this bring forth an even stronger and more powerful system of meridians that will lift humanity and all beings living on this planet to another level in their consciousness development.

Peace with you, peace with us!

7

Exercise to Connect to the Cosmic Pharmacy

The best way to work with the Cosmic Pharmacy is through programming water. You can also work with the Cosmic Pharmacy through your heart and receive the remedies or preparations directly. Through programming water you receive an essence that benefits your whole body, because it spreads through the water with the help of cell intelligence to all the areas of your body that need support or help. The essence obtained in this way will contain absolutely everything that your body, soul, and mind need. Of course, you can also just ask for the specific remedy or preparation that you need.

The number sequence **8787** gives you access to the Cosmic Pharmacy. It is like a key that opens the doorway to this pharmacy for the human community. Access is made possible by the soul of humanity, with whom you make contact via the number sequence **8787**.

In this light-filled pharmacy there are light-filled guardians and light beings who immediately bring you the appropriate preparations and program your water. Or, if you ask them to, they send the preparation directly to your body. These beings are sent by the divine intelligence.

By the way: if you want to program water for your pets, you have to use a different gateway. The number sequence **8787** is the gateway to the morphogenetic fields of humanity alone. We will talk about access to the animal fields later.

Arrangements for the Transfer of Preparations from the Cosmic Pharmacy

Have a glass of water to hand. It should be non-carbonated . . .
And then illuminate your heart.

Let the frequency of gratitude flow into your heart. Feel it. The frequency of gratitude is the first key to connecting to the Cosmic Pharmacy. It has a beautiful golden, pink-white color.

Now connect with the sacred place in your heart. Your intention is sufficient.

Next, visualize the number sequence **8 7 8 7** in front of your heart. You can visualize it in a golden color, but the color doesn't matter. By doing this, you make contact with the soul of humanity, which enables you to access the Cosmic Pharmacy.

Now let a ray of gratitude arise from your heart. Your ray of light penetrates the most diverse dimensions of light and consciousness and the spaces of the cosmic, divine heights.

Now, through the power of your intention, connect with the morphological field of the Cosmic Pharmacy. Then connect with the light-filled guardians and the light beings of this pharmacy. Your gratitude connects you.

Voice your request . . .

"Dear guardians and light beings of the Cosmic Pharmacy!
I ask here and now for the remedies, frequencies, tones, colors and geometrical forms that my body, my soul, and my spirit need.
Gratitude unites me with you.
Time and space are one.
Thank you, thank you, thank you."

Now place the glass of water on your heart. The transfer of remedies takes place immediately. If you would like to, you can keep the glass on your heart for longer. Act intuitively.

Then consciously connect with the water in your glass.

Ask it to record all the healing information. Bless it. Send the love and gratitude of your heart to it. Thank the water.

Thank also the guardians and light beings. Thank the soul of humanity. Disconnect your ray of light from the morphogenetic field of the Cosmic Pharmacy.

Let your heart continue to radiate with the light of gratitude. You can now drink your programmed water sip by sip. It is an essence. If you want to use this essence over several days, you can dilute it with a larger amount of water. One tablespoon to one liter of water is sufficient.

If you feel that you should drink the essence all at once, you can do that too. You can program more water for yourself the following day. We have already told you that the remedies have no side effects and that they have their own intelligence. There is nothing you can do wrong.

After programming, your water will probably take on a different taste. The taste depends on which remedies your water now contains. If you taste bitterness, there are probably bitter substances in it, but that does not necessarily mean that it contains only these substances. It may suddenly also take on a sour or metallic taste. It may taste like herbs or something else you need at that moment. Your water can also change color.

The Cosmic Pharmacy offers all of you countless possibilities. Your chakras can purify themselves with the preparations, frequencies, colors, geometrical forms or tones too. This brings untold relief to your body and organs. Your whole energy level will increase and the consciousness fields of your chakras will connect your individual organs with the cosmic consciousness fields of these organs. Your organs will then be able to communicate again in the language of the individual planets and stars to which they are connected by their matrix.

Every one of you chose a particular planetary constellation for your birth. Every one of you, before your descent to Earth, was in agreement with your karmic plan and with your life on Earth. Every one of you had agreed to your life plan, but for many of you life on this planet is unpleasant because the planetary constellations at the moment of your birth brought great burdens into this earthly incarnation. Every one of you who chose this incarnation has shown, above all, one thing—namely, great courage.

You have chosen this incarnation knowing that unprocessed issues from past incarnations will close your chakras. Chakras, which are energetic entrances to the surrounding cosmic world and the planets that nurture you. Every one of you knew that life on this planet would take place with only partial connection to the cosmos on the energy level.

The planets and stars of your surrounding world make up your matrix system, and their frequencies are like puzzle pieces that fit together to form a complete body image. The influence of planetary frequencies has been overlooked and underestimated by the human community. With each purified chakra, certain organs are reconnected to the planetary community that is responsible for the human being. In this context, the planetary constellation of your birth here on Earth plays, as we have already said, an enormous and indispensable role.

The frequencies and light of the planets automatically connect with the human being to purify their chakras. As colors from the cosmos, they radiate through the chakras and are transported via them to specific organs. As they attract this wonderful light from the cosmic-planetary events, the chakras begin to radiate ever more purely. For example, the planetary frequency of gratitude and harmony, which is primarily associated with the planet Venus, heals and activates your heart. Venus absorbs this frequency from the Divine Source.

Your body is an interaction of your individual organs and your individual energetic systems. Your organs are connected through their consciousness to the cosmic morphogenetic fields of the language of the organs. If you want to communicate with your organs, send them your gratitude. Each organ will then be able to give you detailed information about what it needs at any given time. Each organ has its own consciousness, its own intelligence and its own soul.

The human body has not yet experienced absolute connection to the frequency of the planets and the language of the organs. It has been manipulated and handicapped by dark beings and powers for so long. So far, it has not experienced ease and longevity as it did in those times before the human DNA was manipulated.

The human body will experience a renaissance in the near future. It will very soon be able to recover from the many years of manipulation and the loss of vitality and health.

We will guide you through these steps.

Peace with you, peace with us!

8

Connecting to the Cosmic Pharmacy of Animals

M ost animals living freely in nature have already received their primal frequency from the Divine Source and integrated it into their systems. In this way, they have reached their divine original state of health, naturalness, and vitality.

Nevertheless, programming water is also extremely useful for the pets that live in your household. Pets are mainly influenced by electrosmog. They can also easily take over the negative energies of family members, maybe even yours. They help you through their presence to free yourself of negativities or negative emotions and thoughts. Many pets, especially dogs, develop a wide variety of diseases in the process, often in the form of cancer. They simply take on the negativities of their owners.

If your pets are often ill or you have had pets that died of a certain disease, see if you can change something in your attitude to life. Maybe your dog has developed cancer or you had one that died of cancer? This could have been caused by its basket being placed where there are interference zones.

Before you start the following programming, it is important to know that each animal species has its own higher soul, which is responsible for that particular species.

There are higher souls, for example, for dogs, cats, horses, cattle, or rabbits. Dog breeds also have such higher souls; there is a higher soul of the Dalmatian, Retriever, and Dachshund. For the sake of simplicity, we will work with the higher soul of the species, but not deal with the individual soul groups.

The higher soul of your animal connects it to the associated morphogenetic fields of the Cosmic Pharmacy in the same way that the higher soul of humanity connects you to the Cosmic Pharmacy.

Programming Water for Your Pet

If you would like to program water for your pet, please follow the steps below...

Fill a glass with water and keep it close at hand. Illuminate your heart with love and gratitude. Connect your heart light with the heart light of your animal. If your animal is not with you, it is enough to connect with it virtually.

Then connect with the soul of your animal.

Now let a ray of gratitude arise from your heart. Your ray of light penetrates various dimensions of light and consciousness and the spaces of the divine heights.

Your ray of light connects with the higher soul of your animal. Feel this connection.

The higher soul of your animal now connects you with the light-filled guardians and light beings of the Cosmic Pharmacy of Animals.

Gratitude unites you all.

Voice your request...

"Dear guardians and light beings of the Cosmic Pharmacy!

I ask here and now for the remedies, frequencies, tones, colors, and geometrical forms that the body, the soul, and the mind of my animal needs in this moment.

Gratitude unites me with you.

Time and space are one.

Thank you, thank you, thank you."

Programming is instantaneous. If you like, let the water program itself for as long as your intuition tells you.

Now consciously connect with the water in your glass. Ask it to record all the healing information. Bless it. Send the love and gratitude of your heart to it. Thank the water.

Thank the guardians and light beings once again. Thank the higher soul of your animal.

Separate your beam of light from the morphogenetic field of the Cosmic Pharmacy and from the higher soul of your animal.

Separate yourself on the energy level from your animal.

Let your heart continue to radiate with the light of gratitude. Bless your animal and let its heart also radiate.

You can give your animal the essence you received in this way to drink all at once, or you can dilute it. You can also mix it with its food.

If your animal does not want to eat or drink at this point, then, instead of transmitting the remedy to water, transmit it directly to the heart of your animal or to a specific part of its body. Ask the higher soul of your animal and the light beings of the Cosmic Pharmacy for Animals for this in the same way as in the previous exercise. Act intuitively.

We wish you fulfillment and much success!
Peace with you, peace with us!

9

The Higher Soul of Your Family and How to Work with It on the Energy Level

The time you are in right now is a time that will balance all the existing systems here on Earth until they align with the divine order. All obsolete systems are gradually being transformed into forms that are useful for all human beings. Equality and justice are entering every system on this planet.

For many of you, this time is confusing and allows no feeling of ease. Many of you are wondering where to start and which system you think should be changed first.

We know what thoughts are preoccupying you. We know that you often wonder if your actions on this planet are actually producing concrete results. We understand your concern.

If you really want to achieve concrete results for your future, begin by healing the system of your earthly family. *The family is the absolute foundation for the new positive future! For your future and that of your family and your descendants: heal the system of your earthly family!*

Realize that very often the family systems you see around you no longer offer happiness, energy or support to any of their members. Perhaps you yourself live in a dysfunctional family or one that, for you, is unbearably flawed. This is the rule rather than the exception in your time. Because of the influence of the dark manipulative powers and beings, the state of most family systems is now such that they rarely give any of you reason to be cheerful and happy.

Family members often live in a state of war, of hatred, or in situations where certain members of the family have broken off contact with each other. This is mostly the result of karmic issues. All this lowers the energy of the common morphogenetic field that every family develops. Within its field, each family carries every one of its qualities and abilities, its knowledge, its wisdom, but also any negativities. Every member of the family is connected to this field.

Those human beings who have chosen a better and happier future and have been able to heal their own systems have created new positive fields. They have healed at least part of the morphogenetic field of the whole family with their light and with their positive frequencies.

There is not only a morphogenetic image of a family, however, but also its higher soul.

This higher soul is responsible for every member of the family. It connects the members of the family with each other and wants nothing other than for there to be peace and understanding between them.

We know that relationships within a family are often disturbed or shattered as a result of karma. This may have been triggered by a surge of hatred, envy, malice or other negativity among individual members of the family. At this time, the restoration of family systems is absolutely essential. Such restoration of relationships, if only one step at a time at least at the soul level, brings healing to the whole family.

And this healing is more important than ever right now, because negativities and unprocessed information held in the morphogenetic fields and family systems are implanted into the children of the new generations who are now arriving. That is why now is exactly the right time for the restoration and understanding of the family systems to take place. The family is the absolute foundation!

In the time of Lemuria, when human beings came to this planet, the family was a sacred principle and provided a sacred foundation. It formed a basis for support, a basis for health on all levels, and a basis for loving understanding.

You have certainly done much in the course of your life to heal your personality. That was very good, it was your first and most important step. Now, take the second step and begin to heal the family system of your earthly family with your pure intention.

You came here together so that every one of you can understand the meaning of this incarnation.

You came here together so that every one of you understands that karmic issues no longer belong in this world, in which you as humankind are just ascending into new dimensions of a new positive future.

You came here together so that through understanding you can once again find love in your heart and rise above the karmic issues that may be showing themselves to you more intensely at this time.

You came here together to release these karmic issues once and for all and to begin concentrating on the purest essence that all the members of your family carry within them. Each one of you may be at a different stage of your evolutionary consciousness development, but each one of you, without exception, carries your purest divine essence within you, the essence that unites you all!

You came here together to heal the higher soul of your family. This soul moves forward with you from incarnation to incarnation and rejoices in your every step forward and in your every moment of joy.

Your family is the foundation. Sooner or later, family systems will return to a natural family state without hatred and without malice. Sooner or later, everyone will realize that a healthy, functioning family is the best team they could wish for.

Try to take the first steps for your family and for the higher soul of your family today. Take the first steps and kindle the light in the hearts of your family members. Do not expect thanks or an immediate improvement in the situation. But be aware that any energetic work, truly any energetic work done, is registered by the soul of every single member of your family. The minds of your family members may not register your work at first and you may have the feeling that doing it has made no difference. Trust in the fact that the soul of each one of your family members encodes your work and the light of your deeds. And each soul is thereby given the opportunity to pass on your work to its mind and body at the right time.

With every one of your deeds, with every thought and every positive emotion, you are healing a part of the common morphogenetic field. You are healing and irradiating the light of the higher soul of your family.

No positive thought, emotion or deed is lost. Every positive thought, emotion, and deed joins with other positive thoughts, emotions, and deeds of other light-filled fields and in this way allows the future of your children and the future of the children of the new generations who are now arriving to shine.

To work on your family system as described in the following exercise, it is best if you begin by organizing your thoughts about what has been said in this message—by realizing that through your understanding of your family's karmic situation, you can help to heal a large part of your family system step by step.

Connecting with the Higher Soul of Your Family

In the following exercise we will ask you to connect with the higher soul of your family. We will also ask you to write a few lines of thanks to this higher soul. By doing so, you will be taking a great burden off a large part of your family and your next of kin.

If you are not yet receiving information or signals from the higher soul of your family, you can still do the following exercise and in this way free the soul of your family from burdening emotions in general, without a specific theme. Your intention is sufficient for their healing.

And now breathe deeply and prepare yourself for a conscious connection with the higher soul of your family. Illuminate your heart with the frequency of gratitude. Through the power of your intention, connect with the sacred place in your heart. Feel the gratitude in your heart.

Visualize the number **8 7 8 7** in front of your heart. Visualize it in a golden, pink, and white color.

Connect now with your light beings. Connect with Archangel Michael, connect with Archangel Raphael.

And now speak aloud or in your mind...
"Now and in this space, I call to me all the beings of light who can help me to connect with the higher soul of my earthly family and who can help me to free this higher soul from its burdens.
I accept your help with the gratitude of my heart. Thank you, thank you, thank you."

Illuminate your heart with an even brighter light and let this light rise from your heart into all the spaces and times of your existence.
Observe how the light of your heart expands in all directions.

And now, once more, speak aloud or in your mind...
"I now make contact with the higher soul of my family and the closer relatives of my earthly family.
My light companions accompany me.
Dear soul of my family, please tell me which stressful emotions or stressful programs you suffer from the most and which ones block you the most. I receive every message from you with gratitude.
Thank you, thank you, thank you."

Feel which emotion or information comes to you. Take your time and receive the information that the soul of your family is now sharing with you.

And then speak out loud or in your mind...
"On behalf of my family, I ask your forgiveness for all the negative things that have been done to you. I ask for your forgiveness with all my heart.
I ask Archangel Michael and all the beings of light who can help me to purify the higher soul of my family on the energy level.
I ask Archangel Raphael and all the beings of light who can help me to heal the higher soul of my family to please dissolve all negative burdens in divine light. Space and time are one.
My intention is pure and clear.
Thank you, thank you, thank you."

Now let the light beings do their work.

Send out the love and gratitude of your heart to them. Send out the love and gratitude of your heart to the soul of your family. With this you have taken the first steps toward a healing.

You can now write a few lines of gratitude to your family. For this we have prepared a blank page with the number sequence **8 7 8 7** in all four corners, which you can photocopy as needed.

And you may also like to place four candles in front of you so that your thoughts of gratitude become visible to the light world when you write.

A Sample Letter to the Higher Soul of Your Family

"On behalf of my whole family, I (your name) thank you for accompanying us and existing for us. Thank you for connecting us all through the power of your purest essence and love.

On behalf of my whole family, I ask you to forgive all of us for having wronged you through our actions. In the name of my whole family I ask you for forgiveness in all the times and spaces of our common existence here on Earth.

Thank you, thank you, thank you.

On behalf of my whole family, I thank you for protecting my family here on Earth. I thank you for watching over my family in the heaven of human beings. On behalf of my whole family, I send you light and gratitude for your existence. In the name of my whole family, I bless you. I bless your light-filled home.

Thank you, thank you, thank you."

Through your work for the soul of your family, you are not only helping your earthly family, but also your family in the dimensions of the heaven of human beings.

You are all connected to each other. Which level of consciousness, space or time the individual members of your family are in at the moment is irrelevant. Your family forms a whole, and through the work you do in this earthly state of being, you also heal the souls of your relatives in the dimensions of the heaven of human beings.

Your whole family's morphogenetic field radiates and the negative patterns that burden the whole family and that are passed on from generation to generation can finally be transformed into light.

If karmic issues are truly understood, diseases or programs of addiction—such as alcoholism—within the family can be passed on to the light. Information of a supposedly genetic kind, transmitted from generation to generation, is not necessarily of genetic origin. A newborn baby is still pure and carries the purest divine essence. Its small body, mind, and soul are absolutely pure. But over time, it encounters information within the morphogenetic field of its family that is transferred to its system, such as that of alcoholics.

A child in this family takes on this information. The morphogenetic fields change the structure of its DNA. But there is a way of helping with this on the energy level, which we will tell you about in the following texts.

Become aware that the discord and malevolence in your family are due to the fact that dark forces have been manipulating you for millennia. The consequence and result they want to produce is an unhealthy family environment. Become aware of this and you will save yourself a lot of personal disappointment.

The differing expectations you may have of other family members in the depth of your soul cannot be fulfilled unless you understand that the members of your family are acting according to old manipulative programs that have been fed to them. Stop expecting family members to behave the way you would like them to. This will save you disappointment.

Instead, strive to see beyond their programs. Illuminate these programs and the hearts of the members of your family with light and with your love. Bless them, and, if you sense that your family members are ready for it, talk to them about karmic issues that have literally enslaved them and brought them suffering on a daily basis. Be a shining example to them.

Change your point of view, change your behavior, and change your actions. Be a role model for others and, in time, your positivity will spread to them—step by step, as we always say.

Work intuitively with the higher soul of your family. Help it energetically and in a light-filled manner. And it will gain strength and help you and your whole family—your earthly family as well as your light-filled family in the heaven of human beings.

Peace with you, peace with us!

10

A New Number Sequence
for Regeneration, for Optimal Development, and for the Protection of Your DNA

This time brings with it so many changes and upheavals that we would like to share with you as much helpful information as possible so that your consciousness development can be realized in the best possible way.

All the countless events and situations that are taking place right now expose the human mind to a huge amount of information and perceptual stimuli that the brain must first receive and process. The synapses in your brain are already working faster than they did in 2019, and the receptors that transmit information to the synapses are vibrating faster than they used to. Because of this, information from the outside world can be absorbed and processed by the brain more quickly. The light-filled development of the human being has increased the working of human brain structures. Human beings can now process information from the environment as well as from the light world much faster.

Those who meditate and work on the energy level have often already increased the capacity of their brain's consciousness, thereby enabling a greater number of synapses to form. Their pineal gland has also developed rapidly and created suitable energetic conditions for receiving information from the light world.

Through your light-filled development, your DNA is making great progress, at enormous speed, in the advancement of your body, mind, and soul. In doing so, your DNA is noticeably optimizing itself, this being a result of the light-filled information and impulses from the divine intelligence reaching you more and more quickly. Around Easter 2020, increased light information for the human DNA reached you from the Divine Source. It entered your body through the light chakras above your head. In this way, the first and very successful overwriting of those areas of your DNA that are not directly responsible for the human body but for human consciousness took place.

Your consciousness receives information from your DNA and passes it on to your body. Your DNA, which is identical in its inner structure to the circular structure of the Flower of Life, aligns you on the energy level with the fields of consciousness of this galaxy that are part of the cosmos and divine intelligence.

In the future, human DNA will be able to return human beings to the divine original state of their divine plan, to their cosmic matrix. The regeneration of your DNA will enable your body to have longevity and your consciousness to evolve enormously. Your DNA will be able to regenerate very quickly and reprogram faulty information to the original divine order.

Colloidal gold, which you can obtain in the Cosmic Pharmacy, supports you in helping your DNA to generate a good energy flow. You should also drink as much oxygen-rich water as possible. In the Third Pleiadian Message on the Current Situation from April 2020 ("A new matrix system of galactic order"), we informed you that the divine intelligence has programmed light-filled information into the element of water for the regeneration of human DNA. This means that by drinking water or being in water, you regenerate your DNA and at the same time heal the genetics of your person and your family.

Each one of you is important. Each one of you is an indispensable element in the process of this wonderful ascent. Faulty genetic fields will be reprogrammed and whole family constellations will be restored to full health. Times are awaiting you that are filled with positive changes and adventures.

However, at this time, when development on all levels is taking place at such a great pace, it is still necessary to support the development of your DNA externally and at the same time protect it internally. You are in the midst of rewriting your DNA on the energy level, creating new energetic forms. Negative information from the outside world, especially electrosmog, chemicals in the air and preservatives in food, are very damaging to your DNA and do not allow it to develop in the way that is best for you.

We would therefore like to share with you a combination of numbers that will help your DNA to develop in the best possible way. This enables your DNA to regenerate and receive energetic protection.

This sequence of numbers is **4374**.

Your DNA strands extend beyond the confines of your physical body and absorb subtle, harmful information from the environment. Harmful information and foreign influences as well as toxins make your DNA degenerate, they damage its development, they damage your genetics and ultimately also the genetics of the family members with whom you are in close contact. You are all connected with each other through the subtle information of your DNA.

This number sequence is intended for all those who are sufficiently aware of the situation on Earth to understand when it should be applied. Pharmaceutical preparations that have burdened human beings for many years and undermined the natural function of their organs or parts of their physical material can be neutralized thanks to this combination of numbers—and the physical body of human beings can recover.

This number sequence is not just a string of four digits. Each digit has been energetically programmed by us and linked to morphogenetic fields that have healing and protective effects. Each digit is also connected to fields of colors, tones, geometrical forms, and frequencies, depending on what kind of healing you need at any given time. Behind each of these numbers is a huge number of other number combinations, which are not important for you to know; for simplicity, we have provided you with only these four digits. They contain the whole spectrum of effects.

This number sequence also has a very strong cleansing function and helps your body to eliminate harmful substances such as toxins, chemical preparations or preservatives. You can use it for children who have been vaccinated or given antibiotics. Harmful substances and information will be eliminated from the child's body and the stability of the DNA improved. You can also use them if having chemotherapy or other harsh therapies.

This number sequence supports the regeneration of DNA in general and at the same time reduces its degeneration or aging. Through its combination of numbers it accesses morphogenetic fields created by us, which are guarded by light-filled guardians who, when you use this number sequence, work harmoniously with you, purify your body, and optimize your DNA.

They help your body to be more robust and more resilient to the outside world and its toxins.

It is best to take the color gold for this number sequence; this color helps to rewrite faulty genetic information. Moreover, gold is the color of the future, the color of the Golden Age.

Frequencies coming from the cosmos and received by the human DNA are golden in color. Their influx will continue to increase until eventually all your DNA is sparkling gold.

The light-filled programming of water enables it to bring your body and mind valuable impulses for the regeneration of your DNA. To do this, write the number sequence on a piece of paper with a gold pen. Place a glass of water on this row of numbers and let it work for at least three minutes. Afterwards you can drink the water, slowly in sips.

When using this number sequence, it is always necessary to drink a lot of water, to help your body eliminate toxins and harmful substances. You can also visualize this number sequence, place your hands on it or write it down and keep it close to you. Act intuitively.

Peace with you, peace with us!

11

Bees and Mandalas
to Protect Them

The bees that live on planet Earth come from the planets of the Pleiades. They were brought to this planet in ancient times in order, through their presence and their unlimited, innate industriousness, to connect the Pleiadian civilization then living on Earth with their Pleiadian homeland.

The bees are still connected to their original home. They carry the frequency of the Pleiades star cluster. The honey they produce through their industriousness carries the Pleiadian essence and healing properties.

A large number of different bee species live on our planet. Some of them are much larger than the bees living on planet Earth. They form an independent people with its own intelligence. Some species of these physically larger bees live in areas that serve their spiritual development and preparation for their independent existence on other planets.

Bees are an incredibly industrious and wise people. We call them a people because their intelligence and wisdom are enormous and exceed by far the fields of consciousness of most of the insect species living on planet Earth, to which category we do not wish to assign them. We honor bees deeply.

Recently, there has been an increase in electrical and electronic radiation, which is very harmful to terrestrial bees. Chemical agents used in agriculture are also a threat to bees and their existence. This unfortunate situation will change for the better in the near future, which fills us with joy.

Technologies that use the properties of free energy will considerably reduce electrosmog. Through these technologies, the entire population, the collective existence of humanity and all beings on this planet will be helped. Humanity will be able to use these technologies very soon.

Until then, however, it is necessary to protect the bee people well. Beekeepers who dedicate themselves to the incredibly important work of beekeeping help nature and, above all, human beings, because without the pollination work of bees, yields would be much lower.

Bees love regularity. Bees love everything symmetrical, everything that fits into the divine order. Beekeepers and others who want to help the bees can use mandalas. These heal the energy of the bees and bring them back into the divine order.

Thanks to these mandalas, bees are able, at least partially, to protect themselves from electrosmog. Their energetic signature can then stabilize and their systems are enabled to develop more resistance to harmful substances from the environment.

Bees are very closely connected to the element of air. The patron of the element of air is Archangel Raphael, who can also help them exceedingly well on the energy level if you ask him to do so. They love the energy and the light of the sun. Their connection with Ra, the soul of the sun, is unique.

The best way to help the bees in your garden, or wherever else you find them, is to use the mandala shown here. Its symbolism has a harmonious effect on them. Beekeepers can place this mandala on the bottom of the hive. The signature of this mandala was energetically programmed by us. You can, of course, also use a different mandala for your bees. Act intuitively.

We also advise you to use the number sequence **3717**, which connects the bees with their Pleiadian home. It brings them healing, protective frequencies and the light of their star cluster. You can write these numbers in places where you often see bees, or you can write them near the mandala.

Or you can program water with this number sequence, which you can then use to water the plants that are visited by the bees. The plants pass on the healing frequencies to them.

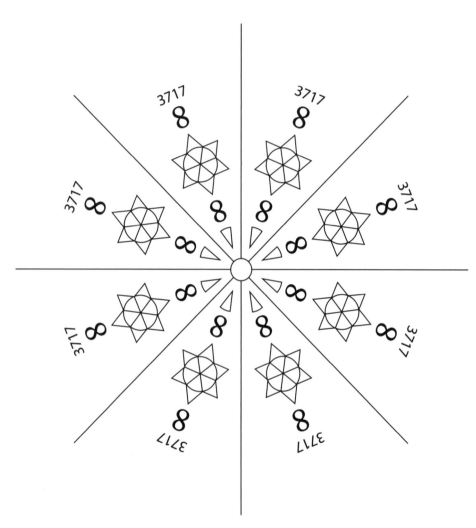

We thank you from the bottom of our hearts for the help you offer to this incredibly important and lovely people.

Peace with you, peace with us!

12

Meditation for all the Children of This Planet

Now I, Orella, would like to give you a short meditation for all the children of this planet. It is for all the children who accompany you, for all the children who are still to incarnate on this planet, and for all the children who have left you.

They left this world because for them it was not a world of joy, happiness, and harmony. They left this world without being granted the attainment of adulthood or youth.

Many children left this world for karmic reasons they had consented to.

But many children have also lost their physical lives in the subterranean constructions of this planet.

Many children have disappeared and been abused.

With this meditation and with these words, I would like to help, above all, those parents whose child has died prematurely or has disappeared without them knowing to this day what actually became of their child.

All those children who left their physical life on this planet found happiness and peace in the heavenly heights. All human children, no matter what their reasons for leaving this planet, have been accompanied by the most beautiful, radiant, and light-filled angels you can imagine.

The souls of human children are very well and happy. All these children's souls were accompanied into the light-filled dimensions. All these children are in the best of hands—the hands of the angelic beings of light.

Human children are the responsibility of the realm of angels, who continually accompany their souls in the light-filled dimensions, who care for them and play with them. In these dimensions the children have everything that makes their souls happy. They are not alone. They are surrounded by angel friends and animal beings.

There, the souls of children who have been wronged during their physical life are given loving healing so that they can come down to this planet in their next incarnations unburdened and without troublesome memories.

Divine intelligence has chosen absolute healing for the memories of these children. Divine intelligence will not allow the dark forces to hurt the souls of these children again.

For all of humanity is evolving in a light-filled manner and ascending into a light-filled future. The manipulation of humanity by the dark beings will end once and for all. Humanity, thanks be to God, has remembered its divine essence and its light-filled existence.

And that brings healing to all of humankind.

The children who are present on this planet have a huge part to play in your positive future.

Together with those children who will gradually be incarnating on this planet, they are creating a consciousness community that will heal the systems of this planet. Children are your future!

Meditation to Connect with the Angelic Beings

Connect wholeheartedly with the angelic beings who are responsible for the human child-being. Your intention is sufficient.

Connect with Archangel Metatron. Connect with Archangel Gabriel. Both are patron saints of children.

Connect with Archangel Raphael, who will help you to heal the children you have in mind.

And now speak aloud or in your mind . . .

"I call all light beings to me and ask them with all my heart to support me in my energy work.

I ask for help for all those children who have left this planet prematurely.

Please purify the souls of these children of their past and heal their memories. Illuminate their past with divine light.

Here and now, I ask for help for all the children who live on this planet. Please purify every child of its difficult past. Purify and heal all these children's systems. Let the burdens and programs they carry, on account of their families and the past generations of their families, dissolve in the divine light.

Illuminate their small bodies, their souls, and their minds with divine light. Illuminate their past with divine light, illuminate their present, illuminate their future.

I now ask for help for all those children who are still to incarnate on this planet. Purify their past, heal their memories. Illuminate their souls with divine light. Illuminate their future on this planet with divine light.

Thank you, thank you, thank you.

I bless all the children of this planet.

I bless the souls of all the children who have left this planet.

I bless the souls of all the children who are preparing for their incarnation.

I bless their past, I bless their present, I bless their future.

I bless their existence.

Thank you, thank you, thank you."

Thank you all for this energy work and this support. Every positive effort heals the whole morphogenetic field of your children—those who have died, the living, and all your future children.

Your love and light heals them all!
Yours, Orella

PART TWO

Messages from the Pleiadians
on the Current Situation

13

Breakthrough into the Positive Future

First message from the Pleiadians on the current situation

channeled on 19 March 2020

Dear messengers of light!

We greet you in this time and in this space and give you information about the situation you are experiencing at the moment.

The situation taking place now was planned in advance. We do not only want to speak about the dark forces and the dark elements as we give you this information. We would like to shed light on the entire energetic situation that is currently taking place.

Many of you will know that by the end of 2018 and the beginning of 2019, the necessary number of people with illuminated hearts and heightened spiritual consciousness was reached.

Many of you most certainly know that their number magnifies their light and illuminates the spaces and times of their existence and thereby also the existence of others.

This light attracts the light of other frequencies that come to you from the cosmos. With each day, the frequency and the light that flows from the universe to you human beings increase.

With each passing day, the consciousness of those human beings who are ready for the development of their consciousness expands. Every day, cosmic portals open, connecting planet Earth with the divine light and its intelligence. Dark-thinking beings understand this situation, and they understand that the present cosmic evolution will inevitably lead to an overall liberation of humanity from the dark energy fields and from the dark past. Dark-thinking beings understand that the anchoring of divine light in human hearts is unstoppable and that, sooner or later, it will spread over the whole planet.

Dark-thinking beings understand that sooner or later humanity will free itself from the clutches of the dark elements and connect to the frequency of cosmic freedom.

What is happening now on this planet is part of a planned action to throw humanity back into the frequency of fear, hopelessness, and anxiety about the future.

This worldwide action is shaking the psyche of the human community, but at the same time it is waking the intuition in human hearts and enabling human beings to spend time with themselves and time with their loved ones.

However, there is something even more important behind this action—and this is the reason why it was planned.

We have often observed how the timelines of the human community have been manipulated. One of these timelines is just coming to an end.

This year's Easter season will be a huge historical milestone for humanity as the current timeline begins to return to its original state.

This year's Easter season brings a great amount of cosmic light to planet Earth, and with it increased Christ light and consciousness.

Those human beings who have prepared themselves for the new cosmic frequencies and have opened their hearts are taking in this new information. This is a great quantum leap into the new dimensions of humanity. This quantum leap in consciousness will help to transform the negative timeline that was supposed to prevent the holistic cosmic consciousness progression of humanity. The human heart is the key and the code for this process.

The overall situation of humankind is beginning to change greatly. Enormous processes are being set in motion that are beginning to create "order" on the planet and to bring the most diverse human spheres back into their original divine state. As things were when humanity came to planet Earth and lived according to the divine laws of purity.

This process, which has basically already begun, will recreate order in everything that is not yet in a state of divine order.

Many of you already carry this divine order in your heart and therefore these changes will not be significant or surprising to you.

For many, however, this situation and its development will be new and will exceed the limits of human expectations and thinking.

We appeal to all humanity and to all people of good will.

Help others who fear their future and expect only the worst. Help them and be an example for them. Show them your positive attitude. Don't let your positive opinions and your joy about the new future be trampled on by the negative thoughts of others.

This upheaval was foreseen a long time ago. It is a breakthrough into the new future. Millions of enlightened human souls on this planet have been waiting for this time. Millions of human souls have incarnated on this plane so that together they can support this upheaval, which will lead to the positive future.

And you are one of them!

The preparations for this upheaval to initiate the new positive future have been going on for decades, centuries, millennia . . . For many of you, it seemed as if they would go on for all eternity . . .

The time that is now dawning brings great and positive changes. Nevertheless, it is necessary to understand that this new, positive future can only come when the structures of the old world have definitely collapsed and been transformed into light.

Although the current situation brings panic and fear to many, it also creates a stronger connection between people who have a pure heart filled with positive intentions.

Many of you have been waiting for this new, positive future for a long time. The dark beings understand the situation and know that with panic and fear they can cover up the unique cosmic event that is pending for the Easter holidays. Through this current situation, webs of fear have been spread throughout humanity.

We, the Pleiadian beings, together with other peace-loving extraterrestrial beings, together with the beings of light responsible for planet Earth, together with the association of human souls of the heaven of human beings, appeal to all human beings of good will—of good will in human hearts:

Do not lose hope in the new future.

Connect with the frequencies of joy, peace, and hope!

Connect with the purest divine essence of the human race. Divine intelligence connects you with the purest essence of the soul of humanity. It connects you with the purest frequencies of divine energy and intelligence. If you like, you can use the numerical code **8787** for this connection. Visualize it or transfer it to water that you then drink slowly, sip by sip.

Thanks to the light in your heart and thanks to your increased consciousness, the negative timeline of humanity can be transformed. Spaces and interstices that no longer belong in the human present and future can also be transformed.

We appeal to each one of you. Connect with your light companions, connect with your family in the heaven of human beings. Your family is making itself increasingly felt from these dimensions. It is looking for increased contact with each one of you! It wants to support you with the light, love, and wisdom carried by your ancestors in the entire energy field of your family line.

This ascent of consciousness, which is moving ahead with each passing day, connects the light of physical and subtle beings.

This ascent of consciousness brings together the physical and ethereal worlds, which unite into one whole!

And it is this process that is just beginning.

Now, in these days.

You are in one of the most significant times in your history.

The dark elements are trying to gain the upper hand over all that is happening in this world, **but the surge of cosmic light coming from the Divine Source is unstoppable!**

Your planet is taking this cosmic divine light into its portals, and the dark elements will have to leave this planet.

The physical and subtle worlds are joining and flowing into each other . . .

Your natural world has started to regenerate at an incredible pace since 2019, because the arrival of the primal frequencies and primal information from the Divine Source is returning nature to its original, natural state.

The state of dormancy that has entered your reality through this unnatural, artificially induced current situation has also helped nature to accelerate regeneration. The globe was able to take a deep breath and begin to gather its strength.

We ask all the inhabitants of this planet to increase their confidence in the positive future of humanity. You have all waited a long time for a positive future, and increased confidence will bring this positive future to you more quickly. Therefore we ask you to support not only yourself but also others through increased confidence in this positive future, gained through your positive overview of this situation.

Every Monday from 9 p.m. to 9.20 p.m. we work more intensively on the energy level with everyone who needs help and with everyone who asks for heightened awareness.

Of course you can connect with us at any other time, but **every Monday from 9 p.m. to 9.20 p.m.** there are thousands of supporters of the cosmic healing frequencies already meditating and working together with us. Together we have created an energy field that helps everyone who needs help. And every one of you—without exception—has access to this field. Your intention alone is enough.

Every Monday from 9 p.m. to 9.20 p.m. we transmit cosmic information and frequencies to anyone who connects with us. Your intention alone is enough. The common positive force between you and us is constantly growing.

And we also support you in other ways: as long as this extraordinarily complicated planetary situation continues, we will transmit cosmic information and energy for you every evening.

We will start doing this immediately: today, 19 March 2020. We will be transmitting these energies more intensively by the end of April. Every evening from 9 p.m. to 9.20 p.m.

Take part. Connect with us.

In the Easter holidays we will transmit energy as well as cosmic frequencies and information even more intensively.

In the Easter holidays, those who are ready for it will receive the light-filled Christ rays that combine in their hearts to form a huge light. And this light will transform the negative times and spaces of the person concerned. The light of human hearts will start a chain reaction among human beings and help to transform the negative timeline and negative reality of this time.

Meditation from the Pleiadians to Raise Spiritual Consciousness

We, the Pleiadian beings and beings of light, would like to share another meditation with you now, one you can do during the Easter holidays.

We, who are responsible for you, will accompany you in your efforts . . .

Sit or lie down comfortably and breathe deeply.

Prepare to raise your spiritual consciousness and receive the Christ light and His consciousness, coming into your heart from the Divine Source.

Ask your soul to connect with the power, beauty, and love of your heart.

Your heart and soul are now one, and your soul is seated in your heart.

Connect with your family in the heaven of human beings through the power and love of your heart and soul.

Now, ask the female line of your ancestors to stand behind you on your left.

Ask the male line of your ancestors to stand behind you on your right.

And now say . . .

"I connect with your love, positive power, and wisdom and with the finest qualities you carry within you. I integrate into my heart these finest qualities, which will help me and other human beings. I thank you for your existence."

Breathe deeply and receive the gifts of your ancestors. Feel their presence.

Now, through the power of your heart, connect with the beings of light and ask them for support in this process.

And now say . . .

"My heart is now ready to receive, integrate, and activate the cosmic Christ light that raises my consciousness and the entire light of my reality."

Take this love and this light into your heart.

Visualize in front of your heart and behind your back in the area of your heart the numerical code **8 7 8 7** .

This numerical code connects you with the purest divine essence of humanity.

And now say . . .

"My heart is connected to the purest divine essence of humanity. My heart receives the cosmic Christ love. The ancestors of my family strengthen and heal my reality.

My heart spreads its light into all the times and spaces of my reality and connects with the light of the realities of other loving human souls.

Light, love, gratitude, and peace fill my heart.

My heart is the key to healing all the levels of my being.

Thank you, thank you, thank you."

Peace with you, peace with us!
Your Pleiadian companions

14

You Are Going through Processes That Will Liberate You

Second Message from the Pleiadians on the Current Situation

channeled on 25 March 2020

Dear messengers of light!

We, the Pleiadian beings, come to you now together with a vast number of other peace-loving extraterrestrial civilizations and beings of light.

We support you within your time and space and transmit frequencies of increased hope, strength, and gratitude into your hearts.

The amplified cosmic frequency of hope will help you to move through the time you are experiencing now.

Hope enables you to connect to the expectations you have developed within yourself during your various incarnations here on Earth.

Your hope connects you with other peace-loving beings who, thanks to never having lost hope, have entered that present where peace and divine, loving laws reign.

The hope you carry within you has never left you and has allowed you to incarnate at this time and in this incarnation on this planet.

Your hope connects you with your new, positive future.

You have waited for this time for so long!

Your soul was occupied by fear for so long!

Your soul has been restrained in the spaces within your body, unable to show its true beauty and greatness, for so long!

Your soul has waited for this time for so long!

Your hope has never run dry and has guided you to this time. To this time, when the bridges that connected you to the dark past are collapsing.

This time will bring wonderful possibilities and tremendous positive changes in the near future, changes that the human mind cannot yet even begin to imagine.

With the arrival of free energy on your planet, incredible possibilities are opening up for your whole community. This will provide material security for the whole of human society.

Planet Earth is just now going through planetary processes that will bring you free energy.

Planet Earth is inexorably approaching the divine order, connecting directly with the line of cosmic orbits that lead to the divine order. Planet Earth is undergoing a huge transformation process.

At the beginning of April 2020, it will begin to pass through the cosmic gateway, which has enormous transformational properties.

Planet Earth is inexorably approaching this gateway. Around the Easter holidays, she will be within the spaces of this cosmic gateway, and the Earth and her citizens will succeed in transforming that which does not belong to the divine order.

Systems that have been artificially created by beings for their own benefit and profit will fall. Because artificially created systems are not divine and loving.

∽

Human beings, do not lose hope; look forward to a positive future, created according to a loving divine order—an order of unconditional love.

This process brings great changes, but it also brings you a peaceful future.

We take great pleasure in telling you that the energy processes taking place are moving us to tears of joy and happiness.

We know, of course, that many human individuals do not understand the actual situation and are distressed by the artificially generated news being presented by the current public media.

Therefore, with today's message we would like to inform you about the energy processes now taking place behind the scenes that are serving the overall process of your ascent.

We have informed you many times that the human community will experience this ascent as a whole.

We have informed you that all human souls, whether they are in a human body, in the heaven of human beings or in other spaces and times, will ascend as a whole.

This common ascent is only possible on condition that the collective consciousness of human beings and the energy processes of the Earth reach a certain level of consciousness.

And this level has been reached!

Planet Earth is currently releasing energies from within herself that do not belong to her natural state. She is detaching herself from programs that have been artificially coded into her and have served to manipulate humankind.

She is dissolving whole energy systems that she has had to carry within her and that have prevented her from entering the natural, divine order.

In these days, the thousands of human souls of those children and adults, who were tormented by the dark beings and therefore met their physical death inside the Earth, have ascended from inside the Earth into the heaven of human beings.

These souls have been liberated—and it is precisely now, in these days, that they are finding their rest and peace.

Light beings are helping them with this transition and healing the emotions they have had to go through. Terrible memories of what their human mind was made to experience are being transformed into light.

Other imprisoned human souls who have spent decades, centuries or even millennia in the interstices of earthly dimensions will also find their heavenly home in the next few days.

Their emotions and memories will also be healed. Give them your blessing so that their transition into the heaven of human beings may be harmonious.

Through the process described above, the human community will be one wholeness at the time of ascent and will succeed in ascending.

Right now, you are going through truly enormous processes that will set you all free.

~

Please do not be unsettled by messages that come to you "from outside," from the artificially created systems. They will not be valid for much longer.

Let the frequency of hope, peace, and joy flow into your hearts. Bless the new positive future that is coming to you.

We are with you, we will accompany you.

Peace with you, peace with us!
Your Pleiadian companions

15

A New Matrix System
of Galactic Order

Third message from the Pleiadians
on the current situation

channeled on 3 April 2020

Dear messengers of light!

We greet you and bring you love, support, and information to help you understand the continuing processes. At the moment, countless processes are in progress, both physical and subtle, and we would like to bring you information that can serve not only your own personal development and bigger perspective, but also the development and bigger perspective of humankind.

The light rays and light information from the cosmos that are entering your solar system are creating a new matrix system of galactic order.

This system is being formed with the help of original divine imprints, and it resonates with cosmic tones that serve to facilitate complete communication of humankind and the living beings of planet Earth with the subtle world and its subtle beings.

This system, thought out by divine intelligence, is absolutely perfect.

The human heart, connected to the crystal networks of the galaxy and to the crystal networks of your planet, receives these tones and this light information.

Your chakras are receiving new light-filled vibrations, and as a result the light-filled vibration of your body is increasing.

Everything is starting to fit together and function properly.

Your timeline, which has deviated from the divine order, is beginning to move in the right direction. Planet Earth will connect to the divine order in the coming days.

In our eyes, this development is unstoppable.

This long-awaited time is just dawning! The light-filled revolution is beginning right now!

Humanity is awakening from its sleep, which has lasted thousands of years. For thousands of years, humanity existed under a veil of forgetfulness, skepticism, and hopelessness.

Humanity is awakening and receiving both information and the support of the beings of light, to help it take the next steps in its evolution of consciousness.

Cosmic lights, helping humanity to remember its essence and its greatness, are coming to planet Earth every day. At the same time, these cosmic lights help you to free yourself from everything that does not pertain to the freedom of humanity.

At the end of March 2020, we were able to observe how your planet was bathed in the beautiful, bright blue light of Archangel Michael. A great many beings of light came at the same time as this blue light, sent to your planet by Archangel Michael. Here they can work more strongly with human beings, enabling them to understand their reality. They help every human being who is prepared to purify themselves on the energy level from the experiences of the past days and weeks.

In these days, your Earth is enveloped in golden, radiant light. This light protects her, and from our perspective it looks as if she is surrounded by beautiful, light-filled cotton wool interspersed with wonderful, light-radiating structures.

Since the last days of March 2020, there has been an intensified reprogramming of human DNA by divine intelligence. A large amount of outdated information that does not belong to your DNA is leaving your planet and its dimensions. The light beings have created intermediate dimensions through which this useless information can pass. Behind the gates of these intermediate dimensions, this useless information is being transformed into light and free energy.

The first light-filled, primal, human DNA information has been reaching you since the beginning of 2019. But now it is coming increasingly from the Divine Source, and divine intelligence is simultaneously encoding this new information, relating to your DNA, into the element of water. *This means that simply by drinking water, information for the reconstruction of your DNA is entering your body! And you regenerate hugely not only through drinking, but also through bathing!*

Divine intelligence helps you in many different ways. It helps you by means of its energy, its light, its love, and its light information. It is sending a great number of light beings to planet Earth to help the human community.

All the prerequisites for entering the new era of humanity have been made available to you by divine intelligence.

It now depends on each one of you, and on how much energy, light, love, and light-filled information you can take into your heart. It now depends on which path your personal manifestation of matter and the new reality takes.

Each one of you is important and each one of you carries the key to the creation of the new positive future in your heart.

Each one of you is the key to the creation of a new positive future!

Now, right now, the actions and decisions you make for this positive future are of the greatest importance!

Right now, the new positive line for your future is being formed.

Through the power of your thoughts and through the power of your heart, encode only the most beautiful things into your future! Through the power of your thoughts and through the power of your heart you are creating the first energetic imprints of the new future timeline of humanity!

Become aware of the power and importance of your thoughts, your feelings, and your actions.

You are creating your new future and your new energetic imprints right now and in this space.

Turn to Archangel Michael and his light helpers to help you purify the experiences of the last years, the last months, weeks, and days. Ask them for release from the artificially created reality.

Meditate and work together with us, the Pleiadian beings, on the energy level, **every evening from 9 p.m. to 9.20 p.m. in your local time**, if you wish. We will work with you every evening until the end of April. And around the Easter holidays, even more. We sent you a meditation for this in the first message of 19 March 2020.

Regular transmissions of our information and energy take place **every Monday from 9.00 p.m. to 9.20 p.m.**

Bless your planet and all beings living on it every day.
Bless all the men of this planet every day.
Bless all the women of this planet every day.
Bless all the children of this planet every day.
Stay pure and positive in your heart.

Your pure heart is the key to your new, inexpressibly positive future.

You are the key.

Peace with you, peace with us!
Your Pleiadian companions

16

The Cosmic Key
to Freedom

Fourth message from the Pleiadians
on the current situation

channeled on 10 April 2020

Dear messengers of the light-filled cosmic information!

We greet you from the cosmic heights and from the cosmic dimensions, levels, and times.

The artificially created processes that are currently taking place on planet Earth are leaving disturbing traces in the hearts of many human beings.

News, publicized by the media, is confusing the minds and disturbing the natural actions and thinking of many human beings who are waiting for their personal freedom. *Personal freedom and its frequencies are reaching into every particle of your existence. Now. At this moment.*

Humankind has been waiting for this to come for a long time. Humankind has been waiting for liberation from the clutches of the dark powers for a long time. This liberation is now taking place and one could say that it is taking place on all levels of the human community.

Even if it is not yet visible to many human beings, liberation is taking place on all levels of your planet Earth's existence, on absolutely all levels.

Your planet has been abused both on its surface and within, and it has suffered great injury, both physical and emotional. Your planet has had to endure the emotions of suffering human beings. It has had to endure the emotions of beings who have hurt human beings.

Now the truth, together with the freedom of each individual, is making its way into all the various parts of the whole existence of humanity here on this planet...and the hidden is coming to the surface.

Those of you who are conscious and pure of heart certainly understand our words.

Those of you who are conscious and pure of heart, help planet Earth and her soul, Gaia, on the energy level. Help the soul of humanity, which has been waiting for this liberation together with you, on the energy level as well.

The soul of humanity has waited so long for this liberation and for its exit on the energy level from the present reality!

The necessary frequencies are now reaching us and every one of you can help! With your positive Earth power, every one of you can help all of us who are involved in the liberation of the Earth—it doesn't matter how you do it.

Today's message is a call to all of you!

Send positive energy and strength to all human beings and all beings of good will.

Support each other energetically by this means!

This year's Easter holidays will bring a tremendous increase in cosmic Christ energy flowing to planet Earth. The increase and manifestation of this wonderful energy will take place through your hearts.

It is not only the planet Earth that is going through the process of ascent. A countless number of other planets and other peace-loving civilizations are preparing for their ascent at the same time. This is also why a multitude of light beings are accompanying all peace-loving civilizations—terrestrial and non-terrestrial.

Your personal participation is of huge benefit to the situation as a whole. The light beings accompany you and help you, but the help that you yourself give is indispensable.

Your help is part of the higher purpose you brought with you to this planet for this time—the purpose you set out to fulfill.

Each one of you is indispensable and every single positive thought of yours, every positive emotion, and every positive deed contributes to the overall liberation of humanity!

Seen as a chain reaction, your liberation also helps the liberation of other peace-loving extraterrestrial civilizations, which in turn contributes to the raising of consciousness and the development of your galaxy!

It is necessary to see and understand the complexities of the whole situation. You are NOT ONLY in the process of the liberation of humanity but also in the process of the liberation of your neighboring populated planets, with which you are connected in frequency. Your galaxy is your common home and you all influence each other.

During these Easter holidays great transformation processes will be taking place, which we have already described in previous messages. Planet Earth is passing through a cosmic portal that will transform everything negative and artificially generated into light or another form of energy.

There is a vast amount of cosmic Christ light flowing to your hearts every second of your present existence, which, thanks to your hearts, is manifesting here on Earth. Your heart carries this light and spreads it into all the spaces and times of your existence. This light connects with other human hearts and other human lights. You are creating a light layer and a light chain reaction around your whole planet.

*You can support this process by strengthening your connection with the frequency of cosmic freedom. The **number 21 is the cosmic key to freedom!** Cosmic freedom is the highest goal of your evolution of consciousness!*

Connect with the frequency of cosmic freedom and all its elements and qualities! Integrate the frequency of freedom into your soul and mind!

Send the frequency of cosmic freedom to all human beings and all beings who need liberation.

Send the frequency of cosmic freedom to planet Earth and to her soul Gaia, so that they receive strength for the time period covering the next days and weeks of their evolution of consciousness. So that they have the strength to free themselves from elements that harm them.

Affirmation for the Attainment of Cosmic Freedom

When working with the frequency of cosmic Christ energy and cosmic freedom, you can use the following affirmation:

"I open my heart and receive light, love, and information of cosmic Christ energy.

Cosmic Christ energy anchors itself in my heart and spreads into all the spaces and times of my existence.

This cosmic Christ energy connects with other pure human hearts.

Now and in this space.

My soul now connects with the frequency of cosmic freedom and absorbs it into its matrix.

I connect through the power of my mind with the intelligence of cosmic freedom and ask it to help all beings who need the frequency of cosmic freedom and who wish to receive the frequency of cosmic freedom.

I ask the intelligence of cosmic freedom for help for planet Earth and her soul, Gaia.

I ask the intelligence of cosmic freedom for help for the soul of humanity.

Now and in this space.

My intention is pure and clear.

Love, light, and freedom spread over the whole planet and help all beings who accept my help.

Now and in this space.

Thank you, thank you, thank you."

And we, the Pleiadian beings, thank you for the manifestation of cosmic information on this planet.

We thank you, and we thank all those beings who have chosen to help planet Earth and humanity in this ascent of consciousness and in the liberation from low-level vibrations and elements. Thank you for your existence! Thank you for your existence on this planet Earth.

Peace with you, peace with us!
Your Pleiadian companions

17

Planet Earth Is Purifying Herself

Fifth message from the Pleiadians
on the current situation

channeled on 26 April 2020

Dear messengers of loving frequencies!

The events happening on planet Earth right now are part of the whole purification process.

The fact that your society is divided into believers and non-believers in relation to the cosmic laws was bound to happen.

Not all human beings on planet Earth are guests from ancient times or from times of the descent of human civilization onto this planet. Not all human beings understand and comprehend this situation.

People with bad or impure intentions will sooner or later no longer be able to adjust to the new, heightened cosmic frequencies of planet Earth. Only a few of them will be able to adapt. Only a few of them will be able to reprogram themselves to the positive in the comparatively short time available to them for this transformation through the new energies. By this comparatively short time we mean a maximum of ten of your human years.

Because the light-filled frequency of your planet will continue to increase, those who do not adjust their consciousness will very likely leave this planet.

Planet Earth is increasing her frequency practically every day. Through doing this, she is performing great feats. And perhaps you have observed that your bodies are also performing great feats and adapting to the vibrations of the Earth.

If you feel tired, let your body rest.

If you feel sadness or any other emotion, simply let it go.

If you feel like crying, let the tears come and cry everything out of your soul that prevents it from being pure. The weeping of human beings is the purest and most natural way of purifying your soul that divine intelligence has given you.

Free yourselves from all the emotions and thought patterns that are being shown to you right now in this more than transparent time.

Your Earth has gone through many eras with you, and through many levels of consciousness. Her overall cosmic evolution is gradually bringing her to the level of consciousness she was in at the time of Lemuria! This was a time of purity of the natural kingdoms and purity of the human community.

Planet Earth is purifying herself so that she can regain her purity completely. She is purifying her surface, and she is purifying her interior. She is purifying the human community.

Dark beings and dark forces are trying to spread their nets, and they want to drag the human community back into systems that they have created here over millennia. With the help of the media, these dark beings and dark powers send out to the human community vast numbers of holographic projections, which cause human beings to believe that the liberation of humanity and the liberation of the soul of humanity is unattainable.

Please do not let yourselves be confused, and trust your intuition. Behind the scenes, countless processes are taking place that are liberating the human community.

Do not lose your faith. With your positive overall view you increase not only your energy but also the energy of the Earth. There are so many things happening behind the curtain that are helping to piece together the mosaic of the whole global process!

The human community is now dividing, but that was bound to happen. Have faith that even those who do not understand the situation at the moment belong to the divine plan and that their stay here on Earth has a reason. These human beings open the eyes of conscious human beings even more. Through the existence of unconscious human beings, those who are conscious gain even more strength and even more determination to change something and, through this, take on responsibility for all of humanity.

The situation that has now arrived will take a quick turn very soon. In the background, processes on both the energy and the physical level are in progress. The results will not be long in coming.

This turnaround will bring a multitude of changes for many human beings.

It brings a deep understanding of all existence to the human mind. This turnaround brings you an understanding of your own personal existence, and it brings an understanding of the meaning of your own personal existence. It brings a deep reprogramming of programs that are not in accord with divine justice and divine harmony.

This turnaround reaches deeply into the soul of beings who have not acted in accordance with divine justice. Divine justice is synonymous with all that is pure, loving, and peace-loving.

You could say that this huge turnaround on the subtle level began at Easter this year.

The physical, visible turning point will soon arrive.

Now, behind the scenes of all that is happening, things are being put in place, step by step, to enable the artificially created systems to take on a new, positive form. Some of these systems will lose their form completely.

We know that the current situation with its artificially created lack of freedom is very difficult for many of you.

Believe that this lack of freedom does not belong to the divine light-filled laws and will not go on for long.

Do not lose your faith and please remain positive. All that is artificially created and does not serve divine justice will indeed leave your planet and your reality very soon!

You are not alone in this process. You are accompanied by light-filled and peace-loving extraterrestrial civilizations. They accompany you in both light-filled and physical form.

Beautiful cosmic Christ light is streaming onto your planet, stabilizing the planet and giving comfort to the human heart in these complicated times.

Open your hearts, and let this light flow into them. This light brings healing, love, and divine justice to the human community.

Your heart is the key to the healing of every one of you. Your heart is the key to the healing of the *whole* human community.

We, the Pleiadian beings, accompany and support you by means of the **daily transmissions of healing energy from 9 p.m. to 9.20 p.m.**

In our first messages in March, we told you that we would be transmitting healing energy every evening until the end of April. To support you in your overall human development, and to support each one of you who chooses to receive the help we offer, we will also transmit this healing energy beyond this time.

Our Pleiadian community has decided to transmit healing energy every evening from 9 p.m. to 9.20 p.m. until we are recalled.

Until such times as we feel that you will no longer need our help.

We are with you, we will accompany you. We carry you in our hearts. Our common reality and common existence with you is beautiful and resembles the shining rays of a clear sun.

The purity of hearts unites us with you and gives us common strength. Helping you gives us incredible joy and fills us with gladness.

You human beings belong to our large family. Our realities are moving closer and closer together and, at some point, the day will come when we will meet each other not only on the consciousness level, but also on the physical level. We look forward unceasingly to this day and to this meeting. And it is precisely this feeling of unceasing joy that gives us the motivation and the strength to continue accompanying you.

We love you. Love is the greatest and most beautiful thing we can all wish for. And our greatest wish is to see you human beings joyful once again and connected with the love of the Divine Source.

This is our greatest wish and also what drives us most strongly in our actions and our help for the human civilization. In each of you we see only the most pure, only the purest essence. And it is precisely this essence that connects us. The pure essence and the pure heart.

We are with you . . .

Peace with you, peace with us!
Your Pleiadian companions

18

The Restoration Has Already Begun

Sixth message from the Pleiadians on the current situation

channeled on 10 June 2020

Dear human beings!

Please have no worries about the future! We are very well aware of the play of feelings in your human soul at the moment. We sense that many of you are worried about what the next days, weeks, and months will bring.

The situation on Earth changes practically from one day to the next. Things are happening that you could not have imagined even in your wildest dreams.

Things that change this time period, this space, and this time forever.

Things that had to come and must come so that the whole mosaic of the time and space of human reality continues to fit together.

Things that every human soul planned before incarnating on planet Earth with the knowledge of how they would play out.

Yes, every human soul planned the course of their present incarnation. Just as you, who are reading these lines right now, did. Every soul. Every one.

Some souls have chosen a positive role.
Some souls have chosen a negative role.
Some souls have chosen a passive role.

But all these human souls knew before their incarnation that this descent to the Earth is part of a huge plan and a subsequent colossal ascent.

Every human soul knew what its task would be before it descended to the Earth.

Every human soul knew in detail how its role would play out.

Even though the transition to the Golden Age is unstoppable, the human community is experiencing times that it has never experienced before in its history. This makes it all the more difficult for any human mind to cope in these times.

From our vantage point, we can safely say that the good will prevail! The human timeline is heading in a positive direction. In a very positive direction.

It is easy for us to move in spaces and times, and we can therefore look at the future of humanity from our standpoint.

Around the Easter holidays this year, the timeline of the human future took the right direction. But this entails purification and restoration of the most diverse systems of the human community. And it applies to systems that have existed on the planet for hundreds or even thousands of years.

These cannot be purified and put right within a few weeks or months.

But the purification has already begun, the restoration has already begun—and although this time is very turbulent, the good will prevail!

No matter what position you are in right now.

No matter what situation you are in right now.

Always remember—the good will prevail.

The takeover and abuse of the human mind, soul, and body will soon be a thing of the past.

*At this moment, through your presence, you are making history. You are writing a new history of humanity and **realizing the new future of humanity!***

You are in one of the most important times of human civilization here on Earth!

The extraterrestrial, negative civilizations are leaving the depths of planet Earth, and its interior is clearing. The higher frequencies of the Earth no longer offer these beings good living conditions. It is not possible for these extraterrestrial beings to ascend to the surface of the Earth and live on this planet. Their systems are not designed for it—not for this kind of breathing and not for this intake of oxygen.

A return to their home planets and home galaxies or an essential reprogramming of their thinking processes and thoughts by divine intelligence, to align them with the positive, will be of vital importance.

The heart of planet Earth will connect with the light of the Central Sun in the coming months, and the wounded interior of Earth will soon be healed by divine light. The soul Gaia will be regaining her full power shortly.

As soon as the interior of the Earth has been healed and cleared by divine light, more and more of the Earth's energy and light will rise to the surface of the planet.

This will result in another wave of increased purification and restoration of the systems of this planet!

You can surely feel that the energy and light of the Earth has greatly increased of late. You can surely feel changes in your mind, your soul, and your body.

As soon as the heart of the Earth connects with the divine Central Sun in the coming months, you will feel the energy and light of the Earth even more strongly! Everything burdensome that does not belong to you will be shown to you even more clearly, and you will have the opportunity to understand all these burdens and issues even better—and to leave them behind you.

And the negative, artificially created systems of human society will be further purified, even more intensively, by divine light.

The truth is inexorably making its way to the surface! Human souls who have chosen a negative role in this incarnation will experience difficult times. For even the most negative human beings know that, although their mind plays this role here on

Earth, their soul will sooner or later decide in favor of their light being and in favor of divine justice.

Even the most negative beings are bound by the laws of light and love.

Even the most negative beings feel their soul deep down and know that, after leaving their body, they will have to answer to themselves for their deeds, in the heavenly realm of human beings.

We can reveal to you already that many of these negative beings will seek redress for their behavior during their stay in these celestial spaces, and will then volunteer to help the human community in the most varied ways.

For in its innermost core, their soul longs for love and light. Please do not forget that many human beings have been manipulated and abused by dark beings and powers. They themselves consented to this manipulation and abuse, but in future times there will be no more room for manipulation and abuse on this planet.

The good and the truth will prevail. The current task of every human being is to not stop trusting, even when worry and fear permeate the most diverse realities of human life.

Always have in mind that the good and the truth will prevail!

We too have gone through a similar time. We interlinked our light and the love in our hearts, time and again, to neutralize the dark elements on our planet. We created huge energy fields of light and love. And these energy fields helped us to find a way out of the difficult situation we were in at the time.

Expand the light of your heart. Your heart connects with other pure human beings. The lights of your hearts will find each other. Distance is of no consequence.

Light and love combine to create a field of divine light and divine love on this planet.

One day, you will wake up and find that the lies, which always contain a dark energy, have been dissolved through the light of your pure hearts. Lies and their dark words are also energy. Dark energy.

147

But stronger than all that is dark and negative is the power of the light and the love of your hearts.

All dark and negative energies will be neutralized through the power of the light and love of your hearts. And you must never forget that.

The good and the truth will prevail.

Peace with you, peace with us!
Your Pleiadian companions

19

The Light Revolution

Seventh message from the Pleiadians
on the current situation

channeled on 29 July 2020

Dear beloved human beings!

The light revolution that began this year is a great step toward raising the consciousness of all humanity. It is part of a chain reaction that is taking place within all the inhabited planets of this galaxy.

Every human being who awakens the light in their heart contributes a ray of light that supports the overall ascent of thousands of other inhabited planets. The humanoid inhabitants of these other individual planets are also undergoing a light revolution of consciousness.

That's right, in total many thousands of planets are ascending from their lower vibrations and aligning with this cosmic event.

The most important step any humanoid inhabitant of this galaxy can take is to understand their own reality and the overall reality of this complex event.

The evolutionary consciousness development of each individual human being and each planet creates a field of light in the form of a spiral. Each planet in this galaxy is going through an individual evolution, but the evolution of all the planets together is striving for the formation of a vast dimensional spiral of galactic consciousness. The consciousness of your galaxy, which offers different spaces and times for the evolution of each individual planet that belongs to it, is fully connected to the consciousness of divine intelligence. The knowledge and information coming to you from the Divine Source permeate the most diverse portals of consciousness that your galaxy has developed.

Helping your human community is very close to our hearts, and the divine intelligences and Cosmic Councils responsible for the individual inhabited planets have been given permission to help. Every civilization that needs help is backed by physical support and support on the energy level from various extraterrestrial, peace-loving civilizations, so that the evolutionary light-filled development spiral does not suffer any flaws or injuries.

Planet Earth is not the only planet occupied by dark forces and dark beings.

Planet Earth is not the only planet that is finding its power and connecting to the cosmic frequency of freedom just now.

Planet Earth is not the only planet on which colossal processes are underway to bring about the complete liberation of all artificially created systems and the liberation of the population!

The light revolution that is taking place right now, and which had to come in the natural course of things, is a significant evolutionary time for humanity.

Humanity is awakening from a very long sleep. It is waking up and beginning to remember the time it lived through before it was artificially sent into a deep sleep—into a deep sleep that dulled all the senses that connect human beings with their divine essence.

This sleep that lasted thousands of years is now coming to an end. And at its end, there is an awakening that allows human beings to remember their essence—to remember their energy, their vibration, their light, and their knowledge.

Your ancestors, who came to this planet long, long ago, are reminding you of your connection with your original, purest divine essence. Your personal ancestral lineage carries within it the information and the connection to the divine essence.

It carries wisdom and experiences from its incarnations here on Earth. Your ancestors, who are speaking out more than ever, are one of the keys that will open the doors for you in your ascent of consciousness. Your ancestors, the first inhabitants of this beautiful planet, hold the key to your memory.

Your connection with your ancestors will allow your heart to radiate and be able to receive information for your development from divine intelligence.

All of your ancestors are connected through beautiful, vast human fields of consciousness. At the same time, they are connected to the soul of humanity—to its love, its light, and its purest consciousness.

And it is precisely this connection of your ancestors with the human field of consciousness that can bring the memory that many human beings are waiting for with so much longing.

It only needs another small part of the population to still remember, for the light spiral of the development of consciousness to increase in size, and for the divine plan of liberation that is currently taking place to be realized.

It only needs another small part of the population for the light revolution to become a complete reality. And we are convinced that, in the course of the next few months, the required number will be reached, so that the necessary information and degree of awareness can be transmitted through the morphogenetic fields to the other inhabitants of the planet and so that then the positive changes, so eagerly awaited, can take place.

The next few months will bring further tremendous cosmic processes.

But the planet Earth is capable of connecting more and more to the cosmic light frequencies and their information—to light information that will bring light-filled impulses for the consciousness development of human hearts and human consciousness.

The earthly portals, of which new ones open practically every day, are absorbing an enormous amount of light into the interior of the Earth. The interior of the Earth is becoming luminous and, in this way, the dark, unhappy past of the Earth is being illuminated as well. All the dark elements within the Earth are now being neutralized in divine light.

Other great processes awaiting humanity have to do with the arrival of ever more rays of light on planet Earth. These rays of light will arrive in the form of a huge spiral of light that will purify the planet on a global scale!

This spiral of light will begin to purify the planet from the end of October 2020. Until then, connection and purification of the globe have been local. Thanks to the spiral form of this ray of light, there will be a global purification on the energy level and correction of everything that does not fit into the divine order of love.

This majestic spiraling ray, which will purify and at the same time nourish the Earth's sphere, brings with it tremendous processes regarding the development of consciousness. It brings changes that will help humanity in the process of finding their lost freedom.

These changes involve major natural transformation processes that may initially cause concern among the people, or feelings of insecurity, or fear about the future. The dark forces here on Earth will in all probability defy this incoming majestic light and fight for their position with their last ounces of strength.

Through this information, we wish to bring words of comfort and understanding to all of you once again. We want you to be prepared for these changes and to know that the positive evolution and positive future of humanity have already been programmed by divine intelligence.

At this time and during the next months, strength and trust in the divine plan—the divine plan that brings love and freedom to each and every inhabitant of this planet who is ready for it—are of course necessary.

At this time, it is more than ever necessary to remain centered, to trust in your own intuition and to connect with your light companions and with your ancestors in the heaven of human beings.

Trust your own plan: the plan that every one of you brought with you to the planet for this time.

Every one of you chose this incarnation and every one of you was in agreement with this colossal plan for the liberation of humanity.

We find it very important to let you know that the next few months will initially bring confusion and turbulent changes. *Nevertheless, these changes are definitely heading toward a positive future for humanity!*

The cosmic frequencies and free energy that have been surrounding you since Easter 2020 will in time bring you a material security that human beings could not have dreamed of even in their most fantastic visions. Humankind will be able to use technologies for the materialization of objects, and this will bring ease and security, thereby banishing fear from the earthly existence of human beings. Technologies that regenerate the human body will bring back health to human beings and cause fear of illness and pain to disappear.

This is why there must be changes that enable outdated, unhelpful, and artificially created systems to be overcome. *The development of humanity is heading in a positive direction. Unstoppable. You are living in one of the most important eras in human history.*

Stay centered. Go out into nature frequently. Connect with your light companions, connect with your family in the heaven of human beings.

Use the number sequence **8787** as often as you like. This sequence of numbers connects you with everything pure that human beings carry within them. It connects you with the purest essence of humanity, which exists in the Divine Source. It helps you to grow spiritually, and it helps you to remember—to remember your purest essence and your plan for this incarnation. It connects you with the divine plan. It binds you to the purest essence and wisdom of your ancestors.

*Visualize this row of numbers—**8787**—in front of your heart and behind your back at the level of your heart.*

Write this sequence of numbers on a piece of paper and place a glass of water on it for at least three minutes. Drink this programmed water throughout the day. Your cells will connect more easily to this numerical code.

You will carry this cosmic numerical code in your system and automatically connect to the purest divine essence of humanity.

You will transmit your frequency through your presence to other inhabitants of this beautiful planet. And not only will you be able to remember—every human being will be able to remember, thanks to you.

Everyone you meet is then given the chance to go through this incarnation, empowered, and centered. They are given the chance to live according to their higher plan.

We wish you much strength, energy, and love as you take the next steps toward your positive future.

We are incredibly proud of each and every one of you.

We love you and our love accompanies you.

We look forward to the time when we will be able to meet you on the physical level.

Your light-filled evolution of consciousness will soon form a connection between us.

We will meet on the spiral part of your consciousness ascent.

Peace with you, peace with us!
Your Pleiadian companions

20

The Great Change

Eighth message from the Pleiadians
on the current situation

channeled on 25 September 2020

Dear messengers of light!

This time brings great changes for the whole human community. Not only human beings, but also animal beings are feeling these changes. The animal beings are programming their fields of consciousness to align with positive waves, and they are allowing the obsolete energetic imprints they lived through in past times to dissolve into light.

Large regions of the kingdoms of nature have already connected to the new frequencies of the dawning Golden Age. Plants and animals are beginning to use the symbolism of sacred geometry, which has become very strongly present again on this planet.

Until now, the Earth's consciousness matrix has been misaligned – it deviated from its original state. The misaligned, deviant matrix has not allowed living beings, plants, and animals, to live their true energetic essence fully and completely. The misaligned, deviant matrix did not allow any population on this planet to live as originally planned by divine intelligence.

The readjustment of the matrix—the planet's network of energy – to its original state, its original form, and its original position took place successfully during the September days of 2020.

The whole planet is now experiencing huge energetic changes. The Earth's core is increasing continuously, in terms of energy and frequency. Rays of energy are emanating from the center of the

Earth, purifying the interior of the planet. *Planet Earth and her heart are preparing for the perfect, energetic connection with the rays of the Central Sun.*

As a result, the energy of the Earth and the greater part of the fields of consciousness of the Earth's soul, Gaia, are currently concentrated within her. Planet Earth will activate energy portals in the coming days and weeks—opening in the oceans, seas, and lakes—that are more than twenty kilometers in diameter. The planet will connect to the consciousness, energy, love, and light of the divine Central Sun through these portals!

This will create a heightened consciousness on planet Earth and accelerate the connection with the fifth dimension of consciousness. It will be easy to perceive the subtle aspects of various regions of the Earth.

Because the Earth and her soul Gaia are preparing for further steps on the energy level and are currently concentrating their energy and consciousness within themselves for a limited time, the Earth will be very vulnerable during these days and weeks with respect to her surface. She currently has no energy and strength left for comprehensive support of the human community. Because of this, humanity is to some extent also vulnerable.

At this time, human help and support is absolutely essential for the Earth and for Gaia! Planet Earth is going through a time of preparation for the majestic, energetic connection with the divine Central Sun!

By the end of 2020, this phase of connection will be completed and the consciousness and energy of the Earth will be distributed everywhere once more. The human community will once again feel the full support of Gaia and the power of the Earth.

The Earth will receive an immeasurable amount of cosmic energy through the prepared portals of the Earth that have already been activated, as well as through the portals that are still waiting to be activated. This cosmic energy will catapult her into new dimensions of consciousness that have already been prepared for planet Earth by divine intelligence.

The consciousness of humankind is also beginning to rise very quickly. For the situation on Earth to be changed for the better, 30 to 40 percent of the population needs to be conscious. When this number is reached, this awakened consciousness will be transmitted via morphogenetic fields into all spaces of the planet and the long-awaited change can then come about. We do not suggest that all the people of this planet will grasp the momentousness of the whole situation. But the number mentioned will be enough for the light to prevail on this planet.

To help you assess the situation, we would like to share with you the development in the percentage of the population that has been awakening over just this period of time.

In July 2020, it was 10 to 15 percent. By September, 23 percent of the population has awakened. Looking at this trend, you can see that the percentage is increasing very quickly. According to our estimation, and according to the estimation of other beings of light who are helping planet Earth, the required number of awakened Earthlings will be reached by the end of the year 2020!

Even though the overall development may seem slow to you, huge changes and processes are taking place behind the scenes of your perception.

The return of the Earth's energy matrix to its original state was one of the greatest milestones and was essential for the overall development of the Earth and its population!

You could say that every day and every night changes happen that contribute to positive development.

We can observe your future from our perspective because we are in the future and your present is the past, seen from our perspective. We are in a different time and space continuum and we can therefore safely tell you that the future of humanity is already positively programmed.

All the energetic imprints that divine intelligence has prepared for humanity and for the future of the Earth already exist.

It is only a question of how quickly the percentage of conscious human beings needed will be reached.

We are convinced that everyone who dedicates themselves to their spiritual development makes up part of this percentage, and with the light and the love in your heart, every one of you contributes to the overall development of the situation of the world's population.

Please pass your light and love on to others.

You are the ones positively supporting the overall situation and helping other inhabitants of the planet who do not realize the momentousness of the whole situation.

You are the ones fully aware of the situation on Earth.

You are the ones who know with what intention you came to this planet.

You are the ones with whom we and an infinite number of other beings of light are working, and to whom we are transmitting light information and support on the energy level, to enable you to continue moving toward your goal—the goal of liberating humanity and the planet from dark elements and beings that have burdened this planet and its population for thousands of years.

The time of liberation has come. The time of liberation and the time for the beginning of the new positive future.

Stay strong. Stay in your power. The next weeks and months could be turbulent. The truth is beginning to come to light. The dark elements and darkly erected constructs will be profoundly shaken.

However, in our view and from our observation, truth and victory are inexorable.

Maintain your confidence and remain positive. This is where your path and your goal are hidden. Soon we will meet in the positive future of your space–time. Soon we will meet on the consciousness level of the newly created energetic matrix of the Earth.

Time and space are one.

Love and goodness will prevail.

Light Meditation for the Energetic Support of Mother Earth

In these days and in the next weeks it will be very important to support Mother Earth on the energy level. Her soul, Gaia, rejoices in every positive thought, emotion, and deed of every awakened human being.

Planet Earth had to endure thousands of years of abuse. Now it is time to thank her for her perseverance, her love, her energy, and her space as the earthly home of your incarnation and to help her.

Planet Earth is in need of your help at this moment. This will enable her transition into new dimensions of consciousness to be accelerated and to proceed more harmoniously. She will be able to regenerate and master the new beginning more easily as a result.

We would therefore like to ask you to be active for Mother Earth. Out in nature is the best place to be if you wish to help on the energy level. If possible, find a place near water.

If you are unable to go outside, imagine it, and give this energetic support wherever you are.

If you are out in nature, find a place that "calls" to you.

Stand in this place and, with your purest intention, choose to help Mother Earth on the energy level.

Breathe deeply, in and out. Your breath connects you with the element of air.

Connect mentally with the element of water—with all the water kingdoms of this planet.

Connect now with the sun in the sky. Through this you connect with the element of fire.

Now concentrate on the earth beneath your feet. On the element of earth.

Then illuminate your heart with golden light.

Visualize in front of your heart the number sequence **8 7 8 7**.

This sequence of numbers connects you with the purest divine essence, which all human beings carry within them. It supports your intention to help the Earth.

Visualize the golden light of divine energy flowing through your crown chakra into your heart.

The cosmic healing light flows unceasingly through your body and through your heart to the heart of the Earth.

Your heart and your intention heal the heart of planet Earth. Your heart and your intention heal planet Earth, and the cosmic light helps you to do so.

The heart of the Earth radiates and is healed.

The heart of the Earth increases in power, energy, cosmic impulses, and information.

Let gratitude now flow out from your heart. Send out this beautiful, loving frequency to the heart of this planet.

And now say . . .

"Gratitude, love, and cosmic light emanate from my heart and heal the heart of planet Earth.

The elements air, water, and fire support the healing of the Earth.

Through the power of my purest intention, I transmit all those elements and all those light frequencies that can be of help to planet Earth at this moment.

The healing of the heart of planet Earth is taking place right now.

Time and space are one.

I bless planet Earth on all levels of her being.

Thank you, thank you, thank you."

Your heart continues to radiate and is nourished by the golden cosmic light.

We thank you for your help.

Peace with you, peace with us!
Your Pleiadian companions

21

Frequencies of Peace

Ninth message from the Pleiadians on the current situation

channeled on 14 November 2020

Dear messengers of light!

Please stay in your heart and do not worry about the future. Please stay in your heart and have done, once and for all, with your personal dark past. Please stay in your heart and let the frequencies of peace and gratitude flow into your heart.

The frequencies of peace connect you with infinite peace and with infinite gratitude. Let these frequencies flow into your system and through this move closer, in terms of frequency, to the Divine Source.

Do not worry about the future. On the contrary. Every one of you is creating their new positive future right now, in this moment. And not only that. All those who are currently illuminating their personal energetic systems are also illuminating the overall systems of this planet.

Step by step you are moving toward the positive future.

Remember that the majority of human beings can still only perceive what is happening around them through the senses of sight and hearing. Remember that behind the scenes, which the majority of human beings cannot yet perceive with their senses, processes are taking place that are helping the human community to win a personal and common victory.

In these days, the number of inhabitants of this planet who have awakened has reached 34 percent. We have no choice but to ascertain with joy that the number of inhabitants who understand the current situation and consciously contribute to the whole spiritual movement is growing all the time. According to our estimates and calculations, the necessary number of inhabitants (around 40 percent) will be reached by the end of 2020.

These are very encouraging prospects, for this number of inhabitants will be a help in ensuring that the positive wave of events neutralizes the dark networks of beings and elements that plague this planet and its population.

Planet Earth is absorbing a huge amount of light with each new day. This is helping to purify the Earth's interior and to connect the heart of this planet absolutely and successfully with the divine Central Sun.

The solar system of which your planet is a part is successfully connecting with other solar systems and with the Central Sun of your galaxy. The spiraling development is leading to positive evolutionary changes that are unstoppable and will take place without human civilization having to do anything.

This is a law of the cosmos and a law of the Divine Source. *The spiraling, light-filled evolutionary development that not only your planet, but billions of other planets in your galactic system, are experiencing is moving toward the laws of light-filled love of the Divine Source and light-filled divine justice.*

Your planet, together with other planets, is ascending step by step to light-filled, loving levels. *The love of the Divine Source is a magnet that lovingly draws the Earth and its population to it.*

In a few years you will look around and realize that this "bad dream" that is currently so prevalent in your reality was one of the last attempts by the dark forces to imprison the planet and its citizens in the third dimension.

However, the unfolding of the light in your heart frees you from this dimension.

Leave outdated reality behind you. Leave dark thoughts behind you. Concentrate on the positive future that is waiting for you right now and approaching inexorably.

Your planet Earth has already taken the first steps toward her positive future. Take steps like these yourself, and connect your heart with the Divine Source—with the Divine Source of love that will definitely free you from the third dimension.

Stay in your heart. Maintain your confidence.

The divine plan is infallible. The divine plan of your positive human future has already been programmed.

Each one of you is a key to a positive future. Each one of you. The key is in your heart. No more, no less.

Be aware of this fact and act accordingly.

Peace and gratitude in your heart help you to emerge from the heavy dimensions, step by step. You are leaving the third dimension. Every positive deed, every positive thought and every positive emotion neutralizes the outdated world of the third dimension.

Your ascent into the fifth dimension of consciousness is unstoppable. You are ascending inexorably.

Affirmation to Strengthen You Energetically

Dear Earth-Soul, dear friend, we would like to give you a short affirmation to strengthen you energetically:

"I am the love of light, and gratitude illuminates my heart.
My reality is permeated with divine light.
The rays of cosmic freedom and purity liberate my soul, mind, and body.
My present and future are absolutely positive and full of love, light, happiness, peace, and divine blessings.
My light beings support and accompany me at all times, and they show me the path that is best for me.
I bless myself, I bless my loved ones, I bless all the beings of this planet.
I bless the planet Earth.
Thank you, thank you, thank you."

We are with you and accompany you.

Every word of this message was positively programmed by us and the light beings.

Every word of this message can heal your heart if you allow it to.

When listening to the message and speaking the affirmation you are automatically connected with the love and light of the Divine Source.

Every single one of you!

> *Gratitude and love connect us.*
> *Peace with you, peace with us!*
> *Your Pleiadian companions*

The Relevance of
Your Incarnation
on This Planet

Closing Words from the Pleiadians

In this New Era you will have the opportunity to work on any issues you may have much faster than before. The year 2020 has brought so much subtle light energy that everything that is energetically dark is now much more visible and perceptible to human beings. Any human being who works on the energy level will be able to confirm this. They will be able to confirm that they have been able to define, recognize, and process dark energies and programs that come to the surface from the depths, more easily.

The light beings have received much additional power in this New Era and can now support and guide human beings more strongly and in a more light-filled manner than before. Thanks to the great intensity of light that is now here on the planet, it will be easier for them to access the human system and its immediate environment. The heart light of human beings also greatly helps light beings to access this earthly reality.

Darkly vibrating patterns in the human system are now literally being catapulted to the surface, one by one. In the New Era, human beings will be able to decide through the power of their intention to either give up these darkly vibrating patterns or turn to those groups of people who have chosen to continue to live their earthly life in their personal third dimension of consciousness. Every single human being has this choice. This is the voluntary decision of every human being.

This New Era brings with it great changes in human thinking. The truth is coming to the surface. The truth will transform an enormous number of fields of consciousness created by human beings within a few months and years. It opens the hearts of human beings, who sometimes experience their incarnation in a consciousness sleep, and it changes the systems of the artificially created constructs of human society. The truth that is inexorably rising to the surface is illuminating the darkest corners of this planet—even its interior. It is opening up a perception of the world with new horizons.

The truth that so many people long for and eagerly await will heal the elements of the dark, manipulative past in human hearts. Truth does not stop at the systems of negatively thinking beings and people. It penetrates them and causes them, in their dark burdened systems, to feel the sense of justice. Divine justice.

Many dark beings and human beings have taken it upon themselves to fulfill the task of a dark-thinking individual in this incarnation. They have taken upon themselves the task of acting negatively during this time and thereby opening the hearts of other human beings who, in their consciousness, are often still asleep, wandering aimlessly through their reality.

Many of these human, dark-thinking beings, who are harming other people and the human community right now, have taken this difficult negative task upon themselves so that, from their present position, they can process the karmic issues of their past times. By taking on the role of a person who is hated by a great number of people because of their behavior and who has to face this hatred, they are processing their karmic affliction. They have taken it upon themselves to fulfill a negative task, but one that helps other human beings to find truth and justice within.

As soon as truth and justice come to the surface, these negatively thinking people will experience unpleasant times here on Earth. And in doing so, they will process their affliction. Ultimately, and from a higher perspective, human beings could be grateful to these individuals for helping through their negative behavior to open the eyes of those who are asleep. All the negative thinking people and beings on this planet have helped to wake up most of the inhabitants of this planet with their negative behavior.

Life on this planet is more or less a "game." A game that is experienced as real. Many of you who are wondering just now what the point of this incarnation is, might agree that life on this planet is one of the many games-in-progress of your existence. Ultimately, you are also consciously present in other worlds, in other dimensions and in other times.

We know that this is difficult for you to comprehend, but your soul and mind only enter into the physical material of your body when the reality of your earthly affairs truly corresponds to your being and when you participate in this game. We know that life on this planet feels real to you, but your true reality is completely different and exists elsewhere. Your reality exists in the divine heights. The divine spaces are your home. Through your incarnation on this planet you have chosen to help the human community as a whole to step out of the third dimension of consciousness development. Through your incarnations on this planet and by dwelling in a human body, you have helped the whole evolutionary development of the human mind.

The game being played on this planet is helping you to fit into the mosaic of the planes of consciousness as well as the mosaic of the planes of new dimensions, spaces, and times of humanity. A correction of human history and a correction of the past of each individual human being is currently taking place.

The game being played right now is helping to dissolve the third dimension of consciousness into divine light. The dark, energetic imprints of human society are dissolving into light, just as the dark, energetic imprints of planet Earth are dissolving into light.

Energetic corrections are taking place every second that allow the outdated imprints of various spaces and times to dissolve into light.

Human beings who have come to this Earth are players who have chosen to take part in this "parlor game."

Every one of you players has taken this task upon yourself. Every one of you is truly courageous.

Every one of you is helping to transform the dark worlds.
Every one of you is indescribably valuable.

⌒

Think of it this way: A new future is being created in every moment. In every moment, the energetic imprints of this planet and the imprints of the human community are changing. Every one of you has a certain field of energy and consciousness around you. This field is flexible. It expands in space and time—depending on what you are experiencing and depending on what you are thinking at that moment. Through this you connect with people who are experiencing the same level of energy and consciousness.

Your dimensions, spaces, and times are all moving. They all shift and connect. Your world looks to us like an energy sphere, which has the most diverse shapes and transparent, polygonal surfaces. These forms continuously connect you human beings anew, and they shift in relation to each other. You all influence each other. You are connected with each other through your own worlds, and these are just merging into one big new world.

The dimensional world on this planet has started to move. One advantage of living on this planet has been the possibility, up until now, of living here in several dimensions of consciousness at the same time. That is why planet Earth has so often been visited by human beings who wanted to work on their personal issues.

Soon, life in the fifth dimension of consciousness alone will be possible on planet Earth. The third dimension will soon be transformed. All its energetic imprints will be transformed into divine light.

The "parlor game" will be over.

Planet Earth will no longer allow any other vibration.

⌒

Those of you who still carry any unresolved issues within you and within your systems have the opportunity now, in this incarnation, to finally let go of them. That is why you came here. To conclude this game. The game of human society that had no fair rules. All of you on this planet right now have chosen to collectively purify and separate yourselves from human history and its dark imprints.

Purifying and neutralizing processes are taking place with every second. The negative energetic imprints that are currently being neutralized look to us like ice floes that are just cracking and breaking up, to then dissolve in the light and warmth of the newly created energetic worlds. The transparent, polygonal surfaces of these energetic worlds are being more and more connected with you human beings, and you can feel that the incoming new energy has an incredibly positive, warming power—and that it is connecting an increasing number of positive people with each other.

Your dimensions, spaces, and times are now interconnecting, and the physical material of your body is absorbing it all. Your body is a means of transport for the realization of new positive times and worlds on this planet. As your mind and soul move in dimensional, spatial and temporal existences, your body here on Earth is taking steps that create imprints for the new future.

Your soul is multidimensional. And your multidimensionality is helping to build a new foundation for the human community. You are not small. You are big. You are greater and more powerful than you can ever imagine.

You are the creators of this world. You are the creators of the reality of the new future of humanity. You are great divine beings who carry the divine light within you. You are God himself. Each one of you carries the light of God in your heart.

The professionalism of your actions here on Earth is ceaselessly leading to changes that have only one goal, the implementation of the divine plan—the neutralization of the third level of consciousness and the gradual creation of the fifth level of consciousness that will connect planet Earth with other planets of similar evolution.

You are powerful and loving in your human heart. It is your heart that shows you the direction in which you should go. Your entire life journey is one huge adventure on this planet—on planet Earth, on which you are currently living through part of your multidimensional existence. At the moment, you are living through an earthly existence. But your true home is much more adventurous and full of light.

Your heart connects you to the adventure and diversity of your light-filled home. Don't forget that. Your heart connects you with your true home and with your inexhaustible primordial power from the light world. Do not forget that your heart connects you to your divine home. Your heart connects you to all that you are. With everything essential. Never forget that.

You are the light and love of the universe.

You are the light and the love of this infinite happening.

You are the light and love of this divine existence.

You are a part of it and it is a part of you.

You are the light and the love of this planet.

You are the light and love of God on this planet.

Your actions and your sojourn on this planet bring divine light to the overall existence of this planet.

Your mind, soul, and body are divine lights that have made their home on this planet.

Your existence is healing this planet.

Your existence is healing humanity.

Do not forget your greatness. Do not forget your light. Do not forget your love.

Love and light connect us and give us joy. We are with you.

We thank you for your existence on this planet.

We thank you for being. For the fact that you exist.

We bless you and we love you.

We now say goodbye to you. We say goodbye only in words. In truth, we will stay close to you. The love and light of our hearts connect us with you.

We wish you continued success. Much strength, endurance, happiness, and joy on this earthly path.

With love!
Your Pleiadian companions

My Current Epilogue

Years ago, when I first contacted the Pleiadian beings telepathically, I received information that I was really not able to understand immediately.

Their sentences still echo in my head to this day. They told me, "What you believe to be humanity's past and history is not true. Human history has been manipulated. What you learned at school is not true. Most events took place differently or never took place at all. Darwin's theory is one of the greatest falsifications humanity has ever had forced on them. The belief in the power of Jesus Christ and other religious movements, adulterated and changed from positive to negative, has divided society and brought about wars. A hunt for ancient knowledge is taking place across the globe. There are civilizations, living in the primeval forests of the Amazon and in subterranean tunnels, of which the general public has so far had no idea . . ."—BAAA!!!

For years, before the Pleiadian beings made contact with me, I had been used to listening to the loving, light-filled symphonies and words of angelic beings. I had been used to hearing about the experiences of non-incarnated family members. I had been used to receiving information from angels and beings of light, as if wrapped in light-filled cotton wool.

The words of the Pleiadian beings were a call, waking me out of this pleasant coziness. Their words and information were incredibly targeted and concentrated, right from the start. In communicating with them, my rose-tinted glasses, through which I had previously perceived the world we live in, fell off. I knew that "something was wrong" on this planet, but was not able to quite grasp it in my

171

imagination and thoughts. I did not understand all the interrelationships that negatively affect human society and basically every one of us too.

Since those first sentences of my awakening, so many concrete things have happened, there have been so many "coincidences," and I have received such a great amount of information, that my view of this world we all consider our home has changed. My understanding of this world and inter-human relationships healed my system. And it took away my fear of the future and of everything that is happening around us—fear of all that was incomprehensible and difficult for me to grasp.

More than ten years have passed since I received the first information from the Pleiadian beings. Their information was always targeted. Their words are always accompanied by the frequencies of compassion and understanding. They don't want us to be frightened by their information. They want us to understand reality. Piece by piece, they share with us information about the "great truth," in easily digestible doses that we are able to take in and process.

When I look back at what has changed for the better for me since then and what has changed for the better for others who have chosen to listen to or read the Pleiadians' words, I see unbelievable progress and positive changes in the systems of life and consciousness. Once you have experienced their healing power, you feel your consciousness lift and your physical sheath begin to heal. Through the presence of Pleiadian frequencies and beings, people who have experienced this connect with cosmic frequencies, with cosmic consciousness and with the cosmic potentials that exist all around us.

When I work with the Pleiadian beings, I am fascinated every time by the fact that they have a solution ready for every situation. They are connected with all the light beings that are responsible for us human beings. In this way, we can find a cure for or a solution to almost any situation that comes our way. The Pleiadians communicate with me directly and without any mincing of words. They do not wrap their words in "pink cotton wool." They know that the right time to help has come—the right time for increased support. They know that human beings need help. Targeted help.

They often tell me how delighted they are that the Cosmic Council and divine intelligence allowed them to enter our systems a few years ago—both our human systems and our earthly ones.

They are not yet allowed to appear on Earth physically or to begin communicating directly with humankind. For now, they are still acting in the background and accompanying us in their light-filled way on the energy level. But this makes what they do no less intensive and comprehensive. They know that the time for increased help has come. In spite of this, they are still giving humanity time to awaken on its own. They accompany us and help us, but the awakening process of humankind must be mobilized by us.

I believe in this and am firmly convinced that humanity is well on the way to achieving it. I believe in it and am convinced that the Pleiadians will soon make direct contact with us. Their spaceships are positioned all around the planet. They are only waiting for the moment when the ray of light from the Divine Source flares up in humanity and the hearts of human beings are able to connect with the Central Source of divine love. Then nothing more will stand in the way, and the first official communication and contact can take place.

I am looking forward to this moment tremendously.

Even though my words may sound like science fiction to many inhabitants of this planet, the future of humanity will be as its pure past—in contact, in peace, and in harmony with other inhabitants of neighboring planets. In times long past, it was possible for us to visit and help each other.

I am firmly convinced that contact will take place very soon.

More than ten years ago, when I had my first mediumistic experiences with the Pleiadian beings, the thoughts I am sharing with you now would have been completely utopian. But now, we are living in a time in which humanity has taken and is taking huge steps in the development of consciousness, steps that were hitherto virtually unforeseeable. Furthermore, planetary and cosmic processes are helping humanity to ascend to these new dimensions, spaces, and times of a light-filled consciousness.

During this time we are not only receiving help from diverse beings of light, we are also receiving essential support from our non-incarnated relatives. In all my seminars, they speak up and offer us their generous help. I am almost always asked to deliver messages and mention the presence of the non-incarnated family of the seminar participants. The words of those who are not incarnated are very powerful and full of understanding.

They say every time, "We are here, we are near you and together with you, and we are accompanying you. Please do not forget this fact. Call us to you, we will be delighted to help. We have insight into your earthly future. We love you."

Lately, the families of our non-incarnated relatives have been receiving increased light-filled strength. Many of the karmic issues that arose due to the manipulated past of humanity could be dissolved in divine light by the light beings. Because of this, the light of our non-incarnated families has increased. Any energy work we do here on Earth also enhances and heals the reality of our family in the heaven of human beings. We mutually support each other.

In some energy work, this leads to experiences that we could never have imagined in the past.

At one of my seminars in Frankfurt, Germany, for example, the group of participants had a wonderful, touching experience. I was leading energy work in which the participants were asking for help for both the female and the male lineage of their ancestors. We connected with the best skills, abilities, and the wisdom of their ancestors. I asked the participants to write their requests and wishes on a piece of paper and then connect with their ancestors, with the purest heart and intention, and allow their ancestors to work on whatever it was they had requested.

This energy work was very powerful and we felt the great power of the family in light.

During the seminar the following morning, we talked about our experiences of the previous day. One participant, Maike, described an experience that moved us to tears. She told us that during the work the day before, she had asked her ancestors for help. She wished she could see her grandson again. She had lost contact with him after an argument with her daughter. The last time she had seen her grandson was five years ago, when he was seven years old. She had suffered a lot, every day.

When she got home after our seminar, she saw there was a missed call on her phone. She called the number back—and on the other end of the line was her grandson! After five years of broken contact, he had called her and said, "Hello Grandma, I wanted to call you and ask how you are." He had found her phone number on the internet.

A few months later, I spoke to Maike again and she told me with joy that she was now back in contact with her daughter too. Both her grandson and her daughter were again in touch with her.

The love and help that the beings of light and the non-incarnated give us is so discerning and tireless that we human beings are often not aware of the extent to which they are actually taking care of us.

It is enough to just accept this help.

It is exactly the same with regard to information from the Cosmic Pharmacy, which I find so very exciting! This information has opened up opportunities for us that we would never even have dared to dream of just a few months ago. In time, constantly shopping for various preparations will no longer be necessary because the gates to the Cosmic Pharmacy and its preparations will have opened for us. We as humankind will be able to connect ourselves to the properties of the preparations and essences that we need. We will then gain access to these infinite possibilities!

This fact, too, has strengthened my conviction that we, as humankind, are on the right track, and that we are returning to the purity of the human soul and to the potential of renewed purity of our origin here on Earth.

Of course, I immediately started experimenting with the Cosmic Pharmacy and, in a group, participants from my seminars and I evaluated the effects of remedies we had received. The results of these experiments were absolutely fantastic. When we concerned ourselves with water, for example, the taste and coloring of it in our glasses also changed. We had all used water from the same source. Everyone tasted their water before and after the programming and the participants described the different tastes and structures of the water.

Many of those participants able to perceive the images of the light world saw the same rooms in this pharmacy, or similar ones. Almost all of them reported that this pharmacy is like a real pharmacy from earlier times. It has dark cupboards and a large desk. In the cupboards are different jars made of brown glass, in which there are various preparations, essences, and herbs. The shelves and cupboards are high and there are ladders to reach them. They also all saw the guardian of the pharmacy.

And everyone in our group received the preparations they needed from these beings of light.

I have also tried out the effects of this pharmacy. When I got up one morning, I felt as if I was going to be ill with a cold and had a rough throat. So I asked the light workers of this pharmacy for help. The next instant, I heard the words "gentian" and "mountain herbs." I saw how they immediately brought different herbs and especially gentian to my glass of water. I then drank this water in sips throughout the day, and on the following day I felt perfectly fit! On the internet, I looked up the effects of gentian. There it said that gentian helps with colds and incipient infections and alleviates fever.

We have tried the preparations of the Cosmic Pharmacy many times already, and each time we were cured very quickly. It is important to remember that not only the preparations but also the different frequencies, tones, colors or geometric shapes needed just at that moment are programmed into the water.

Currently, we are receiving so much help from the light world as to how this information can bring about the complete healing of body, soul, and spirit! We have much better possibilities and conditions for healing than before. Everything is more subtle, more light-filled and vibrating more highly. From now on, we will be connected to other new cosmic frequencies that will give us better insights into different dimensions and spaces. The process of healing is faster. Everything dark that does not belong to us is dissolving into light much faster than in earlier times. Because there is much more light on our planet! Everything that is dark is much more visible and can no longer sustain itself here on Earth and in our systems.

The Pleiadian beings' words—that light attracts light—are even more momentous today than they were in the past. Light attracts light, and the light in our hearts attracts the light of the Divine Source.

Every one of us attracts light from the Divine Source to this Earth with our heart. We attract it into our system, into our family's system.

We are all indispensable. This time needs bright, loving people like you, dear readers.

Human beings like you bring healing to this planet and to humanity as a whole. These are not just words. This is the truth. We are nearing the goal together. We are nearing the truth.

All together. All of us, without exception.

I am happy and grateful for every one of you. I feel your love, I feel your closeness. The light and the love on our planet and in us human beings are increasing and expanding. In every moment. In every instant of our common existence—our common existence on this beautiful planet Earth.

Thank you all for your existence.

I thank you for being.

With love and respect!
Your Pavlina

ADDENDUM

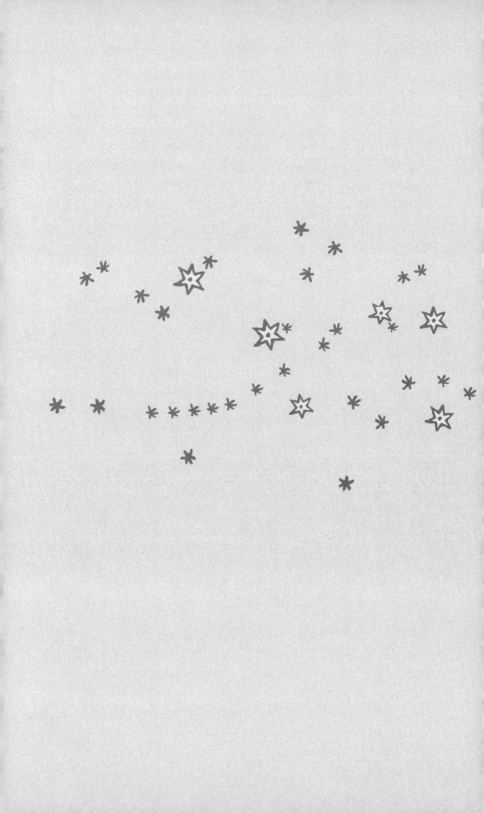

The Crop Circle in
Fischen, Germany

A Message from the Pleiadian Beings
about This Phenomenon

This crop circle of more than a hectare was created in Fischen, near Lake Ammer, which lies south-west of Munich, Germany. Needless to say, I went there as soon as it appeared on 26 July 2020 to receive a message from the Pleiadian beings. It is not the first crop circle in this area that I was able to visit "live."

We greet you in the fifth dimension of your consciousness development!

What you see and feel around you in this crop circle has great significance. Through our Pleiadian energy we have interconnected huge Central European energy nodes that are deep in the Earth. Through doing this, we raised the energy of the energy nodes at the same time.

The light-filled radiance emanating from this structure has a radius of up to eight kilometers and a depth of up to thirty kilometers. If you were to look at the circle on the subtle level, you would see that the energy of its pattern revolves around itself. Its geometry includes parallel lines that raise the vibration of the earth lines we have connected. In addition, this also raises the energy of the crystal networks in the Earth for better communication with us.

When you stand on or near this image, your spiritual awareness increases enormously. The energy of the crop circle raises the vibration of your cells, whose joy in the charged light vibrations is great. This in turn enables you to connect even more strongly with the cosmic energy.

You could say that the whole wide field is shining with light, and therefore all the plants and the soil as well. With a magnetic light. The magnetism created in this field is very positive. It creates a portal of light that provides direct access to the Pleiadian star cluster. But it not only opens a field to the Pleiadian star cluster, it also enables a connection between the Earth's surface and the Earth's interior, as well as a connection between the Earth and its galactic surroundings.

In this way, we have strengthened the entire radiation of the Earth. We call this pattern an "energy stamp," and through its existence it distributes energy, keeping it in a stable position so that it can spread permanently and without outside interference throughout the Earth.

Our communication with you has so far been hidden, but the crop circle contains a message to you. It reads: "Peaceful communication between you and us. Imminent meeting between the earthly and the extraterrestrial civilizations." And a further message of this grain circle is: "Communication between planet Earth and the cosmic light as well as with other populated planets." This tells you that we Pleiadian beings will soon appear to you completely and physically.

At this time it is essential to increase and strengthen the light vibrations of the European states. We did this by connecting the energetic nodal points. This crop circle was created through the harmonious interaction of these nodal points, guided by us.

We have virtually raised the total energy of Europe. This will also increase the spirituality of the human beings here, which will lead to the perception of our first official visits to planet Earth.

Increasing the light vibrations of Germany is of special importance to us. Germany is a very spiritual country; it has a remarkable spiritual past from which many other peoples in Europe and around the world draw. The most diverse knowledge, brought to Earth by this people, is encoded in its soil. The German people are very closely connected with the Slavic peoples and together they form a great spiritual community. Huge morphogenetic fields were created by the spirituality of the German people. Knowledge that was brought to you from the original planets is stored in these fields: knowledge of teleportation, manifestation, regeneration of the body and many other areas of innate human abilities that humanity is searching for and gradually remembering. It was invaded by the dark forces so often because they wanted to use this knowledge for themselves.

It has already suffered terrible punishments countless times for its knowledge. Most recently in the Second World War, for which it was cursed by many millions of people. To this day, the German population suffers from a feeling of guilt and from being cursed on the energy level. It is necessary to bless and strengthen the soul of Germany. She is still sad and has not yet regained her full strength. The soul of Germany appears to us in a feminine form and in a feminine energy. She is beautiful and shows herself to us in a rose-golden energy that she carries within.

Germany has a beautiful, graceful soul and has suffered long enough, together with the German people. She would like to return to her majestic figure and to her full connection with every human being in Germany. The connection of every human being with the soul of Germany would bring relief, strength, and peace of mind to the entire country. The soul of Germany will once again be able to unfold her original greatness and embrace each and every inhabitant of this country so that they remember their origin and recognize their reality.

Many human souls have lost touch with the soul of their own people. Hardly anyone knows that, because of this, they have also lost their connection to the higher soul, which is responsible for the whole of humanity.

The souls of individual peoples are in constant communication with the soul of humanity. They love each other and all souls wish for the peoples to live again as they used to, in peace, harmony, and mutual support.

All the souls of the individual peoples are connected with each other peacefully; there is no competition between the souls of the peoples. All souls, including those of all peoples, are connected through a higher consciousness.

You all know that competition has been created by the dark forces so that human beings are kept separate, and so that they wage wars against each other and fight for the possession or knowledge of other peoples.

The souls of the individual peoples together form wonderfully beautiful, colorful patterns, and this benefits every one of these souls, because the souls of some peoples feel themselves to be in full possession of their power, while others still feel the great pressure that the population has been subjected to by the dark forces.

Connect frequently with the soul of your people to support her power, energy and light! Bless her and bless her healing. If you live in a country that is not your home, support its soul too.

The soul of your current home.

Bless the soul of your people and of the people where you live.

Right now, huge processes are taking place on this planet. The light revolution, which will gift humanity a new, positive future, brings with it great positive changes that will go down in the new, unadulterated history of humanity.

Every human being on this planet has a certain role to play. Every human being has chosen this role. Everyone made their own decision, and it is very wise of every human being to support themselves and their loved ones on this earthly path.

Please forget about competition. Please forget hatred and malice. Return to your essence and your love. This period of time is outstanding and of absolute significance!

Every human being living on this planet is receiving tremendous support from the light world and its beings. Every human being can have as many light helpers for this incarnation as they want and need!

Divine intelligence has developed a plan for the liberation of humankind on this planet. And every inhabitant of the planet was informed of this plan before their arrival. Every one of you is a part of the plan. Every one of you is playing an important role. Even if it seems trivial and insignificant to you now.

Each of you, before your arrival, was connected with the soul of the people into which you were born. Use this connection to strengthen one another! Be aware of the importance of your incarnation here on Earth!

Peace with you, peace with us!

Bonus Affirmations

Affirmation for the Removal of Energetic Implants

"Now, in this space, I allow my Higher Self and all light beings, who can help me, to heal my body, my spirit, my soul and all its parts that belong to my whole existence.

I hereby energetically let go of all negative elements and beings that harm me in any way or negatively influence or manipulate me.

I ask all light beings, who can help me, to completely energetically purify my body, my spirit, my soul and all its parts that belong to my whole existence.

I ask for energetic purification in all times, spaces, dimensions, in-between dimensions, and in all lineages belonging to my whole existence.

I ask for total purification from negative programs and burdens including all existing energetic imprints, duplicates, safety duplicates, and coded programs, as well as all repetitive programs in all spaces and times, dimensions, in-between dimensions, and in all ancestry lineages of my whole existence.

I ask for total purification of the matrix of my soul.

I forgive all who have hurt me. I forgive in all spaces and times of my whole existence. I ask you who I have hurt to forgive me also. I forgive myself. My forgiveness frees us all. In all spaces and times of our joint reality and in our whole joint existence.

I bless myself on all levels of my being.

I bless all humans, beings, and souls who have accompanied me in my existence, who accompany me throughout my present existence, and who will accompany me throughout my future existence.

I explicitly allow only frequencies of positivity, love, and light to touch me. Negative frequencies or those harmful to me have no access to me.

I decide now and in this space in favor of the absolute health of my body, my spirit, my soul and all its parts that belong to my whole existence.

My healing happens now and in this space.

I am absolutely connected with the frequencies of positivity, love, and light. My heart connects me with all healing frequencies of the universe. I am absolutely connected with the positive, healing power of the Earth.

I ask all light beings, who can help me, for absolute protection of my body, my spirit, and my soul. In gratitude I receive the protection, the energetic purification and healing. I am protected, I am pure, I am healed, I am blessed, I am grounded.
Thank you. Thank you. Thank you. Peace. Peace. Peace."

Affirmation for the Reversal of Oaths and Opening the Third Eye

"I hereby neutralize all pledges and oaths that I have ever said or sworn in order to inhibit my clairvoyance, in the divine light. At all times, in all spaces, in all dimensions, in all in-between dimensions, and in all parallel worlds in my entire existence. I neutralize them now and in this space.

I hereby separate myself from all negativity that inhibits my clairvoyance.
I bless all people and all beings that have hurt me. I forgive them. I bless myself, I forgive myself.
My intention is pure and clear.

I hereby activate the function of my third eye and the function of my pineal gland. I connect via my third eye with the intelligence of God and of the light world. Thank you, thank you, thank you."

Acknowledgments

We have now reached the end of another book and this gives me the opportunity to thank all of you in this way—for your support, presence, motivation, companionship and love, and for your strong light. All these elements have been with me throughout this period of writing. I have received them all from my family, my friends, my publisher, and from you, the readers, who are lovingly connected to me on the energy level.

Lately, my family in the heaven of human beings, the group of my ancestors, has been accompanying me to an ever-greater degree. They give me energy and perseverance. But the families in the heaven of human beings are accompanying you all more strongly too, not just me. It is a great gift to feel the connection with the light world of our ancestors. Our common morphogenetic field is becoming brighter and stronger every day.

I am again immensely grateful to my Pleiadian companions for their unceasing information, thanks to which we can increasingly illuminate and heal the common field of humanity.

I am extremely grateful for every piece of information and for every word that I receive "from above."

For me, every word is a gift full of light. Every word brings healing and understanding.

And I finally have the opportunity to thank my daughter Nicole once again from the bottom of my heart for the very successful translation of the text of this book from Czech into German. I would also like to thank my German publisher Michael Nagula for the excellent, professional editing work and for all the organization involved in the publishing of this book. His work is invaluable and brings help and joy to many people. His love for his work is held in this book.

I feel great gratitude in my heart. For everything. For every moment on this planet.

And above all for you allowing me, together with my Pleiadian companions, to virtually re-enter your home and your hearts.

I wish you all, dear readers, much joy, happiness and gratitude on this planet, on which you are currently living through your earthly incarnation.

With peace in our hearts!
Your Pavlina

About Pavlina Klemm

Photo by Melanie Daoud

PAVLINA KLEMM was born in the Czech Republic in the Giant Mountains. At the age of nineteen she came to Munich, where she still lives and works today. Even as a small child she had contact with the light world and, as a young adult, the direction in which her life's journey would take her became absolutely clear.

In 1999, shortly before the turning point of time, she began working intensively with alternative healing methods. Working with the healing universal energy not only developed her own healing abilities, but also increased her connection to the light world and the angelic realm.

Thanks to this connection, she now sees her greatest task is to pass on information concerning universal laws and cosmic developments. The result of her channeling contacts with the Pleiadian civilization is, to date, the book series of *Light Messages from the Pleiades* as well as as a Pleiadian workbook on healing symbols and number sequences. Her card sets and CDs featuring channeled affirmations and exercises are also very popular.

In her seminars, Pavlina caringly accompanies all participants in the spiritual development of their personality and trains them in Pleiadian healing techniques. She not only uses her skills as Lebens-Energie-Beraterin® (Life-Energy-Counselor) from her Körbler training and as a Reconnective Healing® Practitioner from her training with Eric Pearl but also her training by Andrew Blake in quantum healing, her training as a medium of the spiritual world by Doreen Virtue, and her training in Russian healing techniques.

Pavlina continues to devote herself to writing about spiritual cosmic laws, their complexity and their direct influence on our human society, because, as she says, "The teaching and recognition of universal laws is as infinite as the universe itself. It brings joy, awareness, peace and purity to the heart."

For more information and current channelings visit:

https://pavlina-klemm.com

FINDHORN PRESS

Life-Changing Books

Learn more about us and our books at

www.findhornpress.com

For information on the Findhorn Foundation:

www.findhorn.org